Growing In Knowing GOD

A Millennial's Journey In Faith

SADDI WILLIAMS

Acknowledgements

Thanks be to God, the Father of our Lord Jesus Christ, who, according to His great mercy, has caused us to be born again to a living hope through the resurrection of Jesus Christ from the dead.

To my parents, Clayton and Inez Williams, thank you for always supporting me.

To my wife, Mariamah, whose loving and affirming support has made life and family a joy. You inspire me to be better every day.

To my daughter Amoura, you make me proud to be your dad.

To Bishop Donnell Long, my pastor, whose sincere leadership and accountability have provided the encouragement and guidance needed to help me realize this phase of my ministry.

To Scripture Cathedral Ministries – Leadership & Family; my spiritual birthplace and home. Thank you for your loving patience and support. Your understanding and encouragement provided the space for me to mature.

To every friend and family member whose words of encouragement pushed me to see this project through to completion.

I thank God for you all!

CONTENTS

Introduction   1

1. Thy Kingdom, Thy Will   4

2. Sustainer, Deliverer & Guide   7

3. The Father's Passion   12

4. The Father's Patience   16

5. My Weakness, His Strength   20

6. Surrendered to His Care   24

7. All Accounts Settled   28

8. The Turning Point   32

9. A Life Hidden In Christ   36

10. The Secret Place   40

11. A Knock At The Door   45

12. Table For Two   50

13. A Call To Unity   54

14. Sons & Daughters   58

15. Lord, If You Say So   64

16. Fighting Doubt   69

17. All Things Made New   74

18. New Creature, New Direction   78

19. Familiar Foes   84

20. A Heart To Endure   92

21. A Righteous Reward   98

22. Hold Fast Your Confession   103

23. They That Wait   110

24. They That Thirst   116

25. He Who Has An Ear To Hear   121

26. Be Doers, Not Hearers Only   132

27. Whosoever Will   140

About the Author   146

INTRODUCTION

PHILIPPIANS 3:13-14

I'm not saying that I have this all together, that I have it made. But I am well on my way, reaching out for Christ, who has so wondrously reached out for me. Friends, don't get me wrong: By no means do I count myself an expert in all of this, but I've got my eye on the goal, where God is beckoning us onward—to Jesus. I'm off and running, and I'm not turning back. (Philippians 3:13-14 MSG)

Finding God amidst the cloak of culture and the pain of past and present frustrations can become cumbersome. Some have decided to give up trying entirely, while others aspirationally consider growing their relationship with God an admirable pursuit, but no longer necessary.

Through faith in Jesus Christ, I've walked with God for over 26 years. At 39, I've come to learn and experience things I never thought possible. God has a way of orchestrating events to connect with us individually. He is relatable and can speak our language to help us understand Him better. The road to God for some may take time, while others benefit from direct encounters and loving guides. Whichever path you're on, the choice to trust God is always ours. Such was the case in the creation of *"Growing In Knowing God: A Millennial's Journey in Faith."* It began as a weekly burden to write a series of devotions to encourage a community of friends during the season of isolation we endured during the 2020 COVID-19 pandemic.

Weekly scripture reminders grew into a celebration of God's faithfulness. In one day, I received what I felt was the layout for this book. It began with 17 devotions highlighting how God blesses our lives, but it didn't end there. Over 24 months, God revealed Himself through a series of remarkable seasons and experiences. I now see my early inspiration was yet another one of God's invitations to know Him better. I pray that these 27 seasonal reflections bless you as it was transformative for me. The small group for which these reflections were intended initially encouraged me to share this broadly, as they've been inspired to new depths of faith and endurance by it. What began as a six-month e-Bible Study series was a two-year journey full of trial, triumph, and testimony. In the following chapters, I invite you to explore the promises available to us all. I hope this book will serve as a valuable tool in your discernment of God's guidance. You will find a treasure in reading the chapters sequentially, but it is unnecessary. You can begin reading whatever chapter best speaks to where you are now.

"Growing In Knowing God: A Millennial's Journey In Faith" is a collection of reflections I hope will serve as a "savor" to seasoned believers and a "treasure" to those pressing to know who God is. John 17:3 KJV says, *"And this is life eternal, that they might know thee the only true God, and Jesus Christ, whom thou hast sent."*

As you begin, *"Take your time."* No matter where you are on your spiritual walk, be encouraged by your desire to read on. Your desire for God is evidence of His work in your heart *(John 6:44).* Life is full of distractions, as you know; we need God's wisdom to navigate the high tides of prosperity and His grace to traverse the torrents of personal trial. While reading, I hope you find the courage to answer His call by taking the steps that will draw you closer to Him *(Matthew 14:28).* Let us journey together through God's word and into His presence to receive strength to help us stand in our time of need.

2 Corinthians 3:18 NLT

So all of us who have had that veil removed can see and reflect the glory of the Lord. And the Lord—who is the Spirit—makes us more and more like him as we are changed into his glorious image.

ONE

THY KINGDOM, THY WILL

LUKE 11:1

And it came to pass, that, as he [Jesus] was praying in a certain place,
when he ceased, one of his disciples said unto him, Lord, teach us to pray,
as John also taught his disciples. (Luke 11:1 KJV emphasis added)

The desire to communicate is natural to us all at birth; learning HOW to communicate is necessary for each of us—being able to talk is more than learning words; it's learning how to relate. To speak with someone beyond a polite greeting, you must understand who they are and what you have in common. The same is true with prayer. Ecclesiastes 3:11 says that God has "set eternity in our hearts," creating a void that only He can fill. Every disciple desires to communicate with God better; however, many believers struggle with the courage and humility to ask how. *"If any of you lacks wisdom [in anything], you should ask God, who gives generously to all without finding fault, and it will be given to you"* (James 1:5 NIV emphasis added]—the good news: Jesus is still available to give personal guided lessons in prayer.

Matthew 6:9-13 KJV

"After this manner therefore pray ye: Our Father which art in heaven, Hallowed be thy name. <u>Thy kingdom come, Thy will be done in earth, as it is in heaven.</u> Give us this day our daily bread. And forgive us our debts, as we forgive our debtors. And lead us not into temptation, but deliver us from evil: For thine is the kingdom, and the power, and the glory, for ever. Amen"

Before dwelling on what to say, Jesus wants us to understand how to relate. Take a moment, look up, and say," FATHER!".". Instantly, words become less important because the person you're connecting to *you're related to* **(Romans 8:14-15)**. The second thing we must do is ask for God's borders to be extended around our lives. Your father has a Kingdom and borders of leadership that creates a country where nothing is out of his care and control. Your father is the king; no reason or respect is found in wanting to move out and *"find your own place" (Psalm 27:4)*.

Asking for "God's kingdom" is asking for his rulership of our lives. Every day, we are expected to ask for His Kingdom to come because we need more of our life (soul) territory yielded to his protection and government. It's not uncommon for some of us to believe God's word concerning career choices, but we choose our friends without his approval. We acknowledge him in moments of triumph but give in to panic and anger during times of trial; that's what I call the territory of the soul outside the borders of kingdom rule. Don't be discouraged; God is simply awaiting your permission to continue his love crusade of your heart. The more of *"you"* God has, the more *you will possess his will*. The very thought of that reality should fill you with anticipation and encouragement, for this is only the beginning of your conversations. So say whatever you need to talk to your father about today. After all, he already knows what it is; he's just waiting on you to bring it up *(Matthew 6:7-8)*.

"But seek ye first the kingdom of God, and his right-
eousness; and all these things shall be added unto you."
(Matthew 6:33 KJV)

Father, thank you for being God of all. Every good thing concerning me has come from your hand. I want to know and better follow your plan for every part of my life. There are sections of my life where your guidance and influence are easier to see than others. Help me to see the areas of my life and heart you desire to impact next. I desire what you desire for me because your way is best. Grant me the strength I need today to follow your lead. Help me to stir clear of the situations and people that make it difficult for me to depend on your promises. In Jesus' name, Amen.

Two

SUSTAINER, DELIVERER & GUIDE

LUKE 11:1

The following three lines in the Lord's model prayer help us see the Father with deeper appreciation while assisting us with a healthy perspective for the day ahead.

The Sustainer

"Give us this day, our daily bread." While enduring temptation in the wilderness, Jesus recalled an ancient promise that still holds today. *"Man shall not live by bread alone, but by every word that proceeds from the mouth of God" (**Matthew 4:4**).* The request for *"daily bread"* is not limited to our creature comforts; it secures us the grace needed for that day! This grace is the daily cure for our anxiety, or as I call it: "fear of an uncertain future." Depending on what's ahead of you today, this daily grace may come as creativity for a project, wisdom concerning your family, patience to endure trials, or physical strength to meet your daily demands. Remember, your Father knows what we need. He only requires that we ask. Start your day with an entire supply of the Father's Bread, and let tomorrow worry about itself *(**Mathew 6:34**).*

> **Matthew 6:9-13 KJV**
>
> "After this manner therefore pray ye: Our Father which art in heaven, Hallowed be thy name. Thy kingdom come, Thy will be done in earth, as it is in heaven. <u>Give us this day our daily bread</u>. <u>And forgive us our debts, as we forgive our debtors</u>. And <u>lead us not into temptation, but deliver us from evil</u>: For thine is the kingdom, and the power, and the glory, for ever. Amen"

The Deliverer

"Forgive us of our trespasses as we forgive those that trespass against us" (KJV). While anxiety paralyzes us with thoughts of the future, guilt and resentment chain us to the past. Notice that this request is granted conditionally. The Father forgives us to the extent we forgive the wrongs done to us. I admit that this is tough without shame, but all things are possible with God! Jesus said, "Those that have been forgiven of much love the most" *(Luke 7:47)*. In other words, those who have become aware of how MUCH they have been forgiven are more equipped to extend their forgiveness to others. Forgiveness is NOT for the self-righteous; it's the mark of those who have been made righteous *(Isaiah 54:17)*. Forgiveness is the prerequisite to a bright future; without it, you will be trapped in the prison of your past *(Matthew 18:23-35)*.

The Guide

"Lead [me] not into temptation, but deliver [me] from evil" (emphasis added). Please read slowly; here is where we find the first fruit of forgiveness: <u>humility</u>.

Contrary to widespread practice, humility is not having a low opinion of yourself but an *honest opinion*. It takes humility to walk with God, for we must first see Him, then we can align our steps properly. Anyone walking with

God for any time will admit that it can feel more like being carried *(Isaiah 46:3-4)*. It's in God's strength that we live, labor, and find our identity *(Acts 17:28)*. Even on our best day, our good deeds are like filthy rags compared to his righteousness *(Isaiah 64:6)*! Speaking this way or enjoying success with selfless appreciation, may attract some "well-meaning" but misplaced rebukes. The world would say, *"Give yourself some credit,"* or *"You should be more proud of what you've done."*

If you've experienced this, you can inwardly smile, realizing that "any accomplishment" now seen is a fraction of what God is willing to do next. There is no shame in knowing fully where your strength ends and where The Father's begins *(2 Corinthian 12:9)*! Self Awareness is a blessing; it's the wisdom behind the request, *"**Lead me not into temptation.**"* A father knows his child; God's complete knowledge of us enables him to lead us away from "our" temptations. Read what James says about temptation.

James 1:13-14 KJV
"Let no man say when he is tempted, I am tempted of God: for God cannot be tempted with evil, neither tempteth he any man: But every man is tempted, when he is drawn away of his lust, and enticed."

In times of trial, Jesus wants us to put our trust in Him as a faithful Creator to keep us within our limits **(1 Peter 4:19)**. James says we are to rejoice when tempted **(James 1:2)**! We can rejoice because our temptation also serves as reassurance that we are still on the road of life. Triumphant victory over temptation occurs on stable ground with a sincere heart *(1 Peter 4:1)*. So embrace the struggle and cling to God's voice. In every moment of temptation, he promises one of two things: grace to endure and a way of escape. God is our deliverer. He has delivered us from our past and continues to deliver us daily, maturing and preserving us for a glorious future. Your decisions today matter, pray for God's discernment; it's the guidance he provides to keep us away from our weaknesses and living in His strength.

"And since we have a great High Priest who rules over God's house, let us go right into the presence of God with sincere hearts fully trusting him. For our guilty consciences have been sprinkled with Christ's blood to make us clean, and our bodies have been washed with pure water." (Hebrews 10:21-22 NLT)

Lord, thank you for allowing me to see this day. I pray that You bless me to receive and perceive every tool necessary to accomplish Your purpose. Deliver me from the fears and regrets of past mistakes. Guide me to bless someone's day in a way that reflects the love you have shown me. In everything I do, I want to reflect Your intentions; help me not be carried away by my desires. In Jesus' name, Amen.

THREE

THE FATHER'S PASSION

---

1 JOHN 3:16

"We know what real love is because Jesus gave up his life for us. So we also ought to give up our lives for our brothers and sisters." (1 John 3:16 NLT)

In *Luke 15:11-32*, Jesus shares a parable popularly known as *"the prodigal son."* In part, the youngest son demands that their father give him early access to his inheritance. At that moment, he wanted to live his life his way, on his terms, without his father's input, guidance, or cover. Here we see the definition of a *prodigal*. It's not a season of regrettable mistakes, riotous living, or questionable friends; *it's a heart bent on having its way*.

Simply put, a selfish heart is a prodigal heart. One that subtly and continuously tempts us daily to do life as we see it and with only our gain as the goal. The *"Self Life"* is the place where sin begins, where the "micro-rebellions" urge us daily to deny God's suggestions to *"figure things out"* as we go.

There have been times when I've messed things up, big time. I'm not talking about being late for a meeting, mispronouncing a person's name, or missing a payment. I recall seasons where I have allowed myself to be led by a prodigal heart. Looking at life through the lens of *"self"* causes one to misjudge how we see people and circumstances and even question God's intentions. *1 Corinthians 13:4-6* says that real love does not *"seek its own"*; it gives for the good of another. *1 John 3:16* tells us that Christ is the most genuine model we have for unconditional love. A mother's love is strong, but human strength has limits.

> ### Romans 5:6-8 NLT
> **"When we were utterly helpless, Christ came at just the right time and died for us sinners. Now, most people would not be willing to die for an upright person, though someone might perhaps be willing to die for a person who is especially good.** _**But God showed his great love for us by sending Christ to die for us while we were still sinners.**_**"**

Love can be expressed *affectionately* but is defined *"**effectually"*** through the choice to deny self and seek the good. Giving, serving, and sacrificing for goodwill brings glory to God while enlarging our lives. The Father enables us to love because he first loved us. We have security to freely give because He has freely given us all things *(2Peter 1:3)*. In God's presence, there is life and pleasures forever *(Psalm 16:11)*. *"Self"* lives, works and worries alone because it is alone, with no help beyond its own hands to provide for its protection, provision, and peace. It is not the Lord's will for us to worry. He came that we may have life more abundantly! His only ask is to leave our self-care to him and carry our daily tasks with love and trust in Him. In so doing, we will find the love and passion that strengthened Christ to endure his cross for us, which will empower us to carry ours for Him *(Luke 9:23, Hebrews 12:2)*

I pray that we are quick to reconcile with the Father and not run. I pray especially for the moments when the Holy Spirit helps us recognize the areas and times we have drifted from the path due to *"a prodigal"* heart. It happens to us all; a noble task can quickly become more about potential acclaim than our true intentions.

A sudden loss of resources or critical time restraints can cause worry and tempt us to leave off believing in God by going beyond matters we are responsible for. Yes, our gifts and abilities are not without merit, but failure is imminent if God's grace does not help them. Graceless failure is not always immediate, but the longer we handle things our way, the more we continue to drift from the Father's covering. When failure caused by the "self-life" is delayed, it is easy to believe that we have it all under control, unaware of the daily micro-fractures we create in our faith. Those "*faith fractures*" soon make it hard to remember that this perfect God can and will forgive the audacity with which we forget Him. Remember, your Father is the king, and He loves you. There is no debt he can not clear, and his love is unconditional, loving us most when we were most unlovable. Nothing sets his heart ablaze more than to be reconciled with you, even after the most prolonged hiatus.

"So Jesus told them this story: "If a man has a hundred sheep and one of them gets lost, what will he do? Won't he leave the ninety-nine others in the wilderness and go to search for the one that is lost until he finds it? And when he has found it, he will joyfully carry it home on his shoulders. When he arrives, he will call together his friends and neighbors, saying, 'Rejoice with me because I have found my lost sheep.' In the same way, there is more joy in heaven over one lost sinner who repents and returns to God than over ninety-nine others who are righteous and haven't strayed away!" Luke 15:3-7 NLT

Father, your patience has made me aware of areas in my life where I have denied you the driver's seat. I've used the gifts and virtues you gave me to make the best of my life, family, and career as I saw fit. I realize that I need your hand of approval on everything I do; without it, I feel the pressure to perform without the strength to meet my own standards. Your presence erases all regret and worthlessness, seeing that you were always waiting for me to return. Lord, I surrender it to you. Let's do it your way. In Jesus' name, Amen.

FOUR

THE FATHER'S PATIENCE

2 PETER 3:9

"The Lord is not slow in keeping his promise, as some understand slowness. Instead, he is patient with you, not wanting anyone to perish, but everyone to come to repentance." (2 Peter 3:9 NIV)

I thank God for the time that he gives us to grow. As we mature, we begin to appreciate *(in our way)* the goodness of God in how gracious He is to us. God's patience is helped by the fact that he is standing where he knows we will end up. Looking back, we would be amazed to see how He's patiently loved us through seasons where we've ignored Him completely, times when we've been slow or resistant to His direction, or simply immature and clueless. There is a scripture found in the prodigal parable that I've grown to appreciate. *"So he returned home to his father. And while he was still a long way off, his father saw him coming. Filled with love and compassion, he ran to his son, embraced him, and kissed him" (Luke 15:20 NLT)*. The prodigal son had made up his mind to go back home. There were no cell phones in this story and no emails to confirm if the address was still the same; the son headed back to where he and his father last spoke, assured that he would find his father there. Even better, the father was standing looking for his son, anticipating his return. The father saw his son while he was far off in the distance. Patience gave way to passion as the father ran to meet him while still on the road. Can you imagine the walk they shared on the way back to the house together? Life and growth is a process, and the process takes time. That's the patience of God at work. He knows we are growing and desires to walk us through every valley. We allow God to begin the transformation process when we yield our will to Him. So give yourself the grace to grow. We then must adopt the father's patience, knowing He is doing the "perfecting work" for us and in us.

"being confident of this, that he who began a good work in you will carry it on to completion until the day of Christ Jesus." (Philippians 1:6 NIV)

Spending time in the scriptures is like looking in the mirror to smooth out the blemishes we wish to improve. Reading about the children of Israel's wilderness experience, teaches us how it is possible to make seasons of a personal trial last longer than intended. Reading how Peter denied his Lord on the night of Jesus' betrayal should shed light on our hearts' capacity for cowardice. However, be encouraged, just as he prayed for Peter, Jesus also prayed for us *(John 17:19-33)* that even in your stumbles, your faith will not fail but strengthen you to help others see their way through what was once your blind spots. Meditating on God in this way is humbling; God's patience protects us from presuming too much of ourselves *(Romans 12:3)* and being too critical of others *(Matthew 7:1-5)*.

1 Corinthians 13:4-7 NIV

"Love is patient; love is kind. It does not envy; it does not boast; it is not proud. It does not dishonor others; it is not self-seeking, *it is not easily angered*, it keeps no record of wrongs. Love does not delight in evil but rejoices with the truth. It always protects, always trusts, always hopes, *always perseveres."*

1 John 4:16
"...__God is love__...."

Thanks to Jesus, we know *WHO* love is. Love is patient, but it's not passive. Some struggle with the very idea of God because they struggle with understanding His guidance and our need for it. *1 John 14:18* says, *"Mature love casts out fear,"* so let us press on to maturity. Maturity is trusting the one who is conforming us into a masterpiece. A masterpiece takes time; as we endure seasons of heat, molding, and cooling, every stage is beautiful in its own time *(Ecclesiastes 3:11)*. As miraculous as his conception was, even the Lord Jesus had to wait nine months to be born. Losing sight of this can sometimes tempt us to mistake God's character. While doing wrong, we can be blinded to take God's patience as permission. When being "self-righteous," we can interpret God's patience with others as wasted time. God's policy has always been to send his word before sending correction. Judging the rightness of your path solely on the absence or presence of struggle is foolish. It's like waiting for an animal to speak words of wisdom after two human experts have already sent handwritten letters to you on the subject.

So as God is being patient with you, be patient with others. Let's hold each other accountable to the faith, but not hostage to past mistakes. For if we confess our sins, he is faithful and "just" to forgive us of those sins and clean us from the patterns that make falling away happen. Thank God for his patience; by it, He gives us what we need, not what we deserve, and strengthens us for the "now" while preserving us for the "future" *(Jude 1:24)*.

"Now we know that God's judgment against those who do such things is based on truth. So when you, a mere human being, pass judgment on them and yet do the same things, do you think you will escape God's judgment? Or do you show contempt for the riches of his kindness, <u>forbearance and patience,</u> not realizing that <u>God's kindness is intended to lead you to repentance</u>?" Romans 2:2-4 NIV

Father, thank you for a mind to please you. I pray for your forgiveness as I often stumble, and I thank you for showing me those areas where I am most vulnerable. Lord, today I ask for a double portion of encouragement. Help me never forget the "perfecting work" you are doing in my life despite my moments of disappointment. I'm not asking that my tests and trials end quickly, just that I respond properly to learn my lesson the first time around and avoid making this time longer than it should be. In Jesus' name, Amen.

FIVE

MY WEAKNESS, HIS STRENGTH

2 CORINTHIANS 12:9

"And he said unto me, My grace is sufficient for thee: for my strength is made perfect in weakness. Most gladly therefore will I rather glory in my infirmities, that the power of Christ may rest upon me." (2 Corinthians 12:9 KJV)

Paul rightly believed that God could do anything. He prayed and asked God to relieve the burden of a physical ailment. Despite all the miracles he had witnessed done for others, God replied to him with a loving **no**. The Lord's response to Paul explains why no one experiences a *"perfect life."* Jesus said, His strength is made complete when we are finally weak. Weakness, in this case, means our lack of ability, not lack of morality.

God delights in truth, and He expects us to be honest with Him and ourselves **(Psalms 51:6)**. However, it's a real temptation to describe the shortcomings in our character as "weaknesses" simply because we have not yet found victory over them. The weakness that Jesus talks about is the things out of our control. You can be sure that life will bring challenges in which our knowledge, money, youth, or wisdom will be of no effect, essentially making us powerless by our efforts alone. Paul learns to be glad and to Glory in his powerlessness; why? When we are powerless, God is free to do the impossible without any interference from us. Paul glories in the line that separates his effort from God's infinite possibilities. How often is it true that God is just getting started at the precise moment we have reached the end of our rope?

Remember Jesus' sermon on the mount. He said, *"Blessed are the poor in spirit, for theirs is the Kingdom of heaven"* **(Matthew 5:3)**. In other words, you are in the best position when you realize that it's not by power nor by might that things are accomplished, but it's by God's Spirit that things are done **(Zechariah 4:6)**. Those who put no confidence in their efforts will have the reward of heaven's bounty as their supply of strength **(Philippians 4:19)**. The key to this principle is the word *"confidence"*; with whom does your confidence rest? Some misunderstand Jesus' words of "poor in spirit" to mean an expectation of a vow of poverty or believe it ungodly to strive for excellence in achieving one's maximum potential. On the contrary, God expects us to grow and produce great results using the gifts and talents he gave us **(John 15:18)**. The point for us is that we never lose our relationship with God as our true source despite the gifts and skills He's given us.

David was known for his music, but you may have an incredible intellect. Moses was known for his miracles, and you may significantly influence your community. Whatever your gifting is, there is a backside to it as well. Paul was given the gift of great understanding regarding God's plan of salvation, yet he experienced powerlessness concerning his health. God uses Paul's paradox to keep him grounded, never forgetting that only God has all the answers. Despite how much we know, God knows best. No matter how much we can do, God is all-powerful. Proverbs 10:15 says, *"The rich man's wealth is his strong city,"* showing us where his *"confidence resides."* There is nothing wrong with the man being wealthy; his only error is that he solely depends on his wealth to make it through life. God can see if our hearts suffer from this condition. Let us examine ourselves as well, to be sure. After all, it is easy to see how we can soon neglect to pray for the issues we could as quickly pay to resolve. Jesus understood this when he shocked his disciples with the *"rich man vs. the camel"* parable in **Matthew 19:24**. Money and material things have never kept us from God, only our love and concern for them do that **(1 Timothy 6:10, Luke 8:14)**.

The point is simple but only sometimes easy. God can go all the way when we get out of the way. It's marvelous whenever God allows us to participate with him in building our destiny or in being a blessing to others. In such cases, God's goodness is filtered through our level of obedience and faith. Now and then, God allows our weaknesses to surface and sideline us long enough for us to watch Him work unrestrained. Trusting God while *"powerless"* increases our confidence, peace, and dependency on Him like nothing else can. When we enjoy the front-row experience of God's saving grace, we learn to grow beyond focusing on what we have at hand and work to endure to see Him do what we can not do for ourselves.

That is why, for Christ's sake, I delight in weaknesses, in insults, in hardships, in persecutions, in difficulties. For when I am weak, then I am strong. 2 Corinthians 12:10 NIV

Father, life doesn't always feel good, but I know You are. Help me to see beyond my preferences and seek your perfect will. I surrender today's outcomes, breakthroughs, and disappointments to you. Help me grow in maturity, and never forget that the glory is Yours. My inabilities, shorts comings, and failures are not the end of my story but the beginnings of your perfect plan. I claim freedom from the paralysis of perfectionism, it is nothing but fear and pride enticing me to hide. I give you glory through my story. Despite the infirmities of my will and skill, You are transforming me through each moment I trust You completely. In Jesus' name, Amen.

SIX

SURRENDERED TO HIS CARE

JUDGES 7:2

The Lord said to Gideon, "You have too many men. I cannot deliver Midian into their hands, or Israel would boast against me, 'My own strength has saved me.' (Judges 7:2 NIV)

Sometimes God speaks to us through circumstances that feel as extreme as God's request to Gideon. The people we usually depend on are not in a position to help, access to information is limited, and our hearts begin to betray us to fear. Feeling overwhelmed is as familiar to life as it is sudden when it visits us, standing before unimaginable odds. Remember, however, in these moments, we must learn to rejoice in the confidence of God's care. When we are weak, he is strong **(2 Corinthians 12:8-10)**. All that is done for those in God's plan is done so that others may see your response and give your heavenly father credit for raising such a trustworthy child **(Matthew 5:16)**. What you face daily could be more for those connected to you than for you directly. There is peace, courage, and perseverance granted by the grace of God that is contagious to those who witness it practically lived out **(Philippians 4:7).**

2 Timothy 4:16-18 (NLT)

"The first time I was brought before the judge, no one came with me. Everyone abandoned me. May it not be counted against them. But the Lord stood with me and gave me strength so that I might preach the Good News in its entirety for all the Gentiles to hear. And he rescued me from certain death. Yes, and the Lord will deliver me from every evil attack and will bring me safely into his heavenly Kingdom. All glory to God forever and ever! Amen."

Gideon began with an army of about 33,000 troops, of which God dwindled to 300 eligible warriors. Knowing how uneasy this unconventional approach to war was, God made it clear that this victory had nothing to do about Gideon and everything to do about God. The Lord said outright to Gideon; I'm putting you in a position to win so dramatically that there will be no question that I did it for you. The Bible says, *"God gives grace to the humble,"* but the proud He opposes. Surrendering to God's care protects us from the boastful pride that requires God to withdraw his support from us. If our mind is that *"our strength"* is the source of our success, our prayers will never invite God to participate. For our sake, He lets us see the deck stacked against us, beyond our strengths with our weaknesses in clear view, right before He tells us to stand still and see the salvation of the Lord.

2Kings 6:16 NLT

"Don't be afraid!" Elisha told him. "For there are more on our side than on theirs!"

Elisha and his apprentice were in a similar situation, surrounded by an army of soldiers and horses. The young man became anxious and fearful, confused by his mentor's calm demeanor. Elisha prayed to encourage and teach his protege about their shared security in God's care. *"Lord open his eyes, so that he may see"* (**2 Kings 6:17**). The older man replied, you see, son, there are more with us than they that be with them. Immediately, the young man could perceive the thousands of angels from heaven's army surrounding the enemy surrounding them.

The Lord has promised that he will never leave or forsake us and will always be with us, even until the end of the world. What a fantastic promise! Perhaps you find yourself fighting to meet seemingly unrealistic expectations; your heart is concerned with family matters, or you're uncertain about tomorrow's challenges. The battle is not yours, it's the Lord's; remember, *"greater is He that is in you, than he that is in the world"* (**1 John 4:4**). We're never against the odds when we have God. While the Lord fights our battles, our conflict is winning the war against fear, disbelief, and self-reliance. That is why we must always remember His promises.

"And I give unto them eternal life; and they shall never perish, neither shall any man pluck them out of my hand. My Father, which gave them me, is greater than all; and no man is able to pluck them out of my Father's hand. I and my Father are one." <u>John 10:28-30 KJV</u>

Lord, thank you for being the shade upon my right hand. I stand to face the day because I know You already won the battle. Every thought of fear, anxiety, and worry I take prisoner now and make it obey the promises you've given me in your word. Give me the faith I need today to see your saving hand work on my behalf. Show yourself strong today, not only for me, Lord, but for every life connected to me. Let it be known that there are more standing with Your believers than those who trust in the world. In Jesus' name Amen.

SEVEN

ALL ACCOUNTS SETTLED

JOB 42:10

And the Lord turned the captivity of Job, when he prayed for his friends: also the Lord gave Job twice as much as he had before. (Job 42:10)

CRISIS *(noun):* a time at which a significant change occurs, the turning point of a disease, indicating either recovery or death - the 'decisive point.' A time when a difficult or important decision must be made.

Job would be one if there were ever a human model for faithful endurance through struggle. Job acquired and accomplished much in his life, but he is most remembered by how much he'd lost. By human standards, Job lost everything except his faith. With faith that endures, Job gained more than a "double portion" but a better perspective; that though life is hard, God is always good. Indeed that is much easier said than lived, but Job did it. As devout as he was, Job's faithfulness to the Lord was not without its measure of self-interest. Even when asked, satan himself accused Job's devotion as a means to garner and maintain good health and fortune **(Job 2:3-5)**. Don't underestimate how easily the heart can stow away undetected presumptions in the human soul for years. We should be cautious if we regard "being a good person" (religious) as a noble goal, achievable without God's help. Job's friends also had this erroneous view and, with it, failed miserably at any attempt to provide any comfort to their friend in a time of crisis. Job's good friend Eliphaz said:

"Stop and think! Do the innocent die? When have the upright been destroyed? My experience shows that those who plant trouble and cultivate evil will harvest the same." (Job 4:7-8) NLT

Such a remark is spiritually tone-deaf. However, we must never forget what this sounds like. At the first sign of distress, our emotions and intellect will betray us if we are not aligned with the Spirit of God. Our *"natural side"* can not comprehend spiritual things **(1 Corinthians 2:14).** If left to ourselves, we become superstitious at best without God's grace. Paul experienced the same reaction when he was shipwrecked near the island of Malta in Acts 28. A snake had bitten him once he came ashore; for this to happen after surviving a shipwreck, the people that looked on Paul feared that he may have been a murderer being justly punished by cosmic justice. After observing Paul for a while and seeing that he suffered no ill effects, they swung to the opposite extreme, thinking perhaps that he was a God instead.

The promise we must hold to is the truth that Job and his friends eventually came to understand. God will never leave or forsake us, even when it seems like your world is ending. He wants your devotion to be for love's sake, with a free heart, not an arranged marriage of balance sheets and quid pro quo. God is not an unknown entity waiting to be appeased but a loving father we should desire to please. There are benefits to walking with God **(Psalms 103:2),** but whatever God does or allows in our lives, it's never done to us, it's done for us, despite how unhelpful it may seem along the way. Our responsibility is not to build credit with God but to *grow in the faith that allows God to build his credibility with us.* God shows his hand in the trials, and the triumphs of life, the key to receiving His grace is in the heart of our response.

Galatians 6:1-2 NLT

"Dear brothers and sisters, if another believer is overcome by some sin, you who are godly should gently and humbly help that person back onto the right path. And be careful not to fall into the same temptation yourself. Share each other's burdens, and in this way obey the law of Christ."

The turning point for Job is the turning point for us. We become free to do God's will as we turn our gaze from our situation. We are most like God when we decide to forgive a legitimate debt or wrong. Forgiveness is heaven's formula for salvation; let us not be stubborn in finding an alternative route. Jubilee is a celebration every 50 years, where debts are forgiven, and accounts settled. Our personal Jubilee can begin whenever we trust God's way of doing things. His kingdom is perfect, with no one suffering loss. The Lord's Jubilee brings joy; the gladness of the one whose debt has been forgiven is only second to the person who can forgive a debt without losing any gains.

"If you forgive people their sins, your Father in heaven will forgive your sins also. If you do not forgive people their sins, your Father will not forgive your sins. Matthew 6:14-15 NLV

Lord, I want to experience your peace and freedom fully. I thank you for paying the price for my sins, but I need your help in what to do with the sins I have endured at the hands of others. I know you are a righteous God, but I've grown to a place where praying for justice is insufficient. My heart needs to be justified. The areas that have been made crooked by cruel offenses can be made straight by Your grace. By faith, I know that you can make me whole, give me the strength to forgive [call out their names] and free me to walk in your fearless love. In Jesus' name, Amen.

EIGHT

THE TURNING POINT

1 JOHN 2:1-2

"My dear children, I am writing this to you so that you will not sin. But if anyone does sin, we have an advocate who pleads our case before the Father. He is Jesus Christ, the one who is truly righteous. He himself is the sacrifice that atones for our sins—and not only our sins but the sins of all the world. (1 John 2:1-2 NLT)

Perhaps it's a blind spot in our perspective, a soft spot in our emotions, or a stubborn streak in our souls. Whatever the cause, from time to time, we get it wrong. It's disappointing, especially when our intentions to *"do better"* are sincere, and our labor is for noble reasons. It's even more discouraging when we fully intend to take the *"I Road"* instead of the *"high road."* It all begins with a voice that screams, *"I want," "I need," "I feel," "I DESERVE."* This trap is as old as the Garden of Eden and just as strong.

Paul reveals something incredible in 2 Corinthians 5:18; *"**God has given us a ministry of reconciliation**."* By Jesus Christ, God provides the perfect plan for imperfect people. A ministry of reconciliation gives us the means to turn back to the Lord whenever we have drifted off course. Consistent and loving,

God is Father to the prodigal and married to the backslider. No matter where we may find ourselves, God's position has never changed *(Deuteronomy 30:14)*, and His thoughts toward us remain the same *(Jeremiah 29:11)*. Since the beginning, God has left breadcrumbs for every generation to find our way back home to Him. King Solomon built a temple to the Lord at the height of Israel's glory and devotion. However, God knew there would come a time when His people's hearts would stray, and their lives would wander the *"I-Road"* away from Him. Even while times were good, God instructed the faithful on what to do for the "bad days."

> **2 Chronicles 7:14 NLT** *(emphasis added)*
> *"Then if my people who are called by my name will humble themselves and pray and seek my face and **TURN** from their wicked ways, I will hear from heaven and will forgive their sins and restore their land."*

Repent is another way of saying **TURN**. Turning is what God requires so that salvation can happen. We are continuously being saved by faith in Him, turning from our reliance on things and people and seeking God's way of doing things. In Acts 2:38, Peter declared passionately and clearly, **"Repent** (Turn/Change your mind) *and be baptized everyone one of you in the name, Lord Jesus Christ for the remission of your sins"* *(emphasis added)*. I know it's popular to declare *"No Regrets,"* and I agree with the sentiment regarding learning and growth. However, a life without regrets is a life without repentance. It's presumptuous to think we don't make mistakes or ever will. Some go as far as not believing in the concept of sin at all, rationalizing our quirky imperfections as the result of circumstances, or just *"being human"* absolves us from the natural course of consequences. I've found this reasoning to be a subtle trick of the enemy, designed to set us up for shame and despair through an inevitable future stumble. In truth, whoever says they have no sin, is only lying to themselves *(1 John 1:8)*.

So the question is, "*How do we respond **when** we mess up?*" David gives us one of the most candid examples in _Psalms 51_. After being confronted with a personal misdeed, David made no excuses but began to make amends with God and the people he hurt. David was humble, sincere, transparent, honest, and passionate! David walked close enough to God to know that the Father would never reject someone with a truly sincere and repented heart, no matter how big the mistake. David was what we should aspire to be in our repentant prayers.

Hebrews 4:14-16 NLT
So then, since we have a great High Priest who has entered heaven, Jesus the Son of God, let us hold firmly to what we believe. This High Priest of ours understands our weaknesses, for he faced all of the same testings we do, yet he did not sin. So let us come boldly to the throne of our gracious God. There we will receive his mercy, and we will find grace to help us when we need it most.

Be encouraged; God knows that we are prone to mistakes, believe He has made a way of escape through Jesus Christ. In so doing, we leave the perfecting to Him *(Psalm 138:8)* while daily receiving the grace for our pressing toward perfection *(Philippians 3:14)*. Whenever we feel convicted, we feel compelled to run rather than to reconcile. There is no reason to fear, your heavenly Father loves you, and He understands your struggles and knows your breaking points. God desires that we run to him, get it right, be healed, and set back on course to fulfill His plans for us. As incredible as God is, He is amazingly detail oriented when it comes to ours hearts *(Luke 12:7)*. An unaddressed conviction can quickly spoil into feelings of condemnation, which is not Godly at all. God isn't angry if it's been a while since you've sincerely prayed. He's waiting for you to **TURN**.

Seek the Lord while he may be found; call on him while he is near. Let the wicked forsake their ways and the unrighteous their thoughts. <u>Let them turn</u> to the Lord, and he will have mercy on them, and to our God, for he will freely pardon. (Isaiah 55:6-7 NIV)

Father, I want to bring before you [state situation/incident]. I confess that my actions/attitude at that moment does not reflect who You are nor who You've called me to be. Father, renew my mind and heart to see situations as you see them. Cleanse my heart from the triggers that cause me to lose self-control and succumb to fear. For those I've offended by my actions, comfort them. If possible, grant me the space and opportunity to reconcile with them directly. Thank you for being faithful in your forgiveness and blood, cleansing me from all unrighteousness. In Jesus' name, Amen.

NINE

A LIFE HIDDEN IN CHRIST

COLOSSIANS 3:2-3

Think about the things of heaven, not the things of earth. For you died to this life, and your real life is hidden with Christ in God. (Colossians 3:2-3 NLT)

What comes to mind when you think of *The Resurrection*? Is it only a triumphant historical fact, a future-blessed hope, or perhaps both? I'm sorry if it sounds like I am using "*religious words*"; there is no other way to describe it. *Resurrection power* is the most distinctive attribute of God's plan of salvation, his character in the face of obstacles, and his effect on our everyday lives. <u>Romans 8:11</u> declares, *"And if the Spirit of him who raised Jesus from the dead is living in you, he who raised Christ from the dead will also give life to your mortal bodies because of his Spirit who lives in you."* Insight into Colossians 3 shows a trade involved in this transformation. In our case, the old life, with its short-sighted desires and fears, is given up so that we can live out God's intentions through our everyday life.

In <u>John 10:18</u>, Jesus states powerfully that the life He has hidden in the Father is beyond anyone else's reach but His. He said, *"No one can take my life from me. I sacrifice it voluntarily. For I have the authority to lay it down when I want to and also to take it up again. For this is what my Father has commanded"* (*NLT*). The Father commands that we *"put off our old self and its deeds"* (**Ephesians 4:22-24**) to fulfill what the Spirit of God desires to do through us day by day; "putting off the old man" must be done voluntarily. The power of the cross of Christ is seen in the display of love's volition. He did it willingly. Only by our love for Him can we <u>willingly</u> deny ourselves and take on His nature *(1 Peter 4:1)*. There is no better life to live than *a life that gives life*.

> <u>**Galatians 2:20 KJV**</u>
> **"I am crucified with Christ: nevertheless I live; yet not I, but Christ liveth in me: and the life which I now live in the flesh I live by the faith of the Son of God, who loved me, and gave himself for me."**

The closer we walk with the Lord, we become more sensitive to His promptings and guidance. Our goal should be as simple and profound as Enoch's testimony; <u>Genesis 5:24</u> states, *"Enoch walked with God."* Our experience, of course, doesn't end there; it gets better. God walks with us, for all who the Spirit of God leads are the children of God *(Romans 8:14)*. This leading has an incredible impact on us and everyone we're meant to encounter. <u>Philippians 2:13</u> <u>(NLT)</u> says, *"For God is working in you, giving you the desire and the power to do what pleases him."* God's working in us explains the desire towards spontaneous acts of service, writing a letter of thanks, privately paying a tab, and giving a hug or words of encouragement. When divinely inspired, such moments evoke tears of relief and joy, smiles of comfort and confirmations, or speechless amazement followed by the question, *"**How did you know?**"*

Romans 12:1-2 NLT

And so, dear brothers and sisters, I plead with you to give your bodies to God because of all he has done for you. Let them be a living and holy sacrifice—the kind he will find acceptable. This is truly the way to worship him. Don't copy the behavior and customs of this world, but let God transform you into a new person by changing the way you think. Then you will learn to know God's will for you, which is good and pleasing and perfect.

God's impact on your life is what makes you peculiar. What he does for us frees us to do for others in like manner. By the grace of God, we put our selfish ambitions aside, allowing God's will to take center stage. At that moment, we become extensions of God's intentions, ambassadors of His country, extending the borders of God's care to those we encounter. Paul was so impacted by the new life God gave him that he devoted his life to enabling others to see and know God as we as they could *(Philippians 3:10)*.

"You are the light of the world. A town built on a hill cannot be hidden. Neither do people light a lamp and put it under a bowl. Instead, they put it on its stand, and it gives light to everyone in the house. In the same way, let your light shine before others, that they may see your good deeds and glorify your Father in heaven." **Matthew 5:14-16 NIV**

Lord, help me today to be a blessing in someone's life by supplying a need or being an answer to prayer. Father, you know what we need, I don't need to know their issue. I only need to know your voice and what you require me to do to make someone's day. I want my actions to be divinely inspired, whether to do much or little. Help me to be obedient to your Spirit's leading today. Whether my actions are done anonymously or randomly, let them confirm your love for that person. In Jesus' name, Amen.

TEN

THE SECRET PLACE

PSALMS 91:1-2

He that dwelleth in the secret place of the most High shall abide under the shadow of the Almighty. I will say of the Lord, He is my refuge and my fortress: my God; in him will I trust. (Psalm 91:1-2 KJV)

Over time, phrases often spoken become regarded as cliché or "figures of speech," with the meanings of their origin usually becoming lost. An old antiques show once aired on television where novel items were appraised. People brought in their family items and heirlooms that once belonged to a great-grandparent or family member. After close inspection from a trained expert, some people learn that there is great value in the item they hold. Some exclaimed, "*How could this old thing mean so much?*"

I've often pondered the same thing regarding phrases and statements made by my elders, who have walked with God much longer than I have. Despite what natural wealth they may or may not have accumulated, their praise and testimonies are strikingly straightforward and humble. With blessed assurance and contentment of soul, I would hear older saints testify how grateful they are to God for "*keeping them.*" They would add, "***Thank the Lord for keeping*** *me from all hurt, harm, and danger."* This cliche had to grow on me until I realized how precious such a declaration this is. Only those alive, loving God, and depending on his care, can declare such treasured truth. Saints who have found this treasure have seen God's *secret place*. In my youth, I always smiled at the phrase, thinking of it as a funny way of saying the same thing in three different ways. In time I better understood the depths of God's keeping power.

He Will, Keep You From All Hurt

Psalm 147:3 KJV
"He healeth the broken in heart, and bindeth up their wounds."

In Luke 17:1, Jesus reveals an unavoidable experience in life. He said, without a doubt, there will come a time when we are offended. An offense is a deeply personal or emotional hurt, painful enough to tempt us to sin by looking for ways to avenge ourselves. Psalms 147:3 gives us peace in knowing that there is no earthly sorrow that heaven cannot heal. That is a secret, best left to time to help us understand. The Lord is rich in mercy and love, able to make good any bad debt. Forgiveness demands no explanation or repayment from the offender, instead, it places the bill at God's feet (Luke 17:2-4). *God shields us from becoming jaded by hurt and distrustful emotions with this knowledge.* We are free to shed the judgemental facade, extending the same grace we've received from God to others. We can not do this independently; when we rely on our efforts, we don't become strong, but rigid and brittle. Only by the Spirit of God will the Father accomplish the promise of Ezekiel 11:19-20.

And I will give them one heart, and I will put a new spirit within you; and I will take the stony heart out of their flesh, and will give them an heart of flesh: That they may walk in my statutes, and keep mine ordinances, and do them: and they shall be my people, and I will be their God. (Ezekiel 11:19-20 KJV)

He Will, Keep You From All Harm

Psalm 91:7 NLT
Though a thousand fall at your side, though ten thousand are dying around you, these evils will not touch you.

Job, amid his trial, confessed that a human born of a woman has only a few days to live, and yet they are full of troubles *(Job 14:1)*. We live in uncertain times, where the love of many has gone cold. The daily news is full of murders, robberies, and riots, yet life must go on. Paul reminds the believers in Ephesus, *"So then, be careful how you walk, not as unwise people but as wise, making the most of your time because the days are evil" (Ephesians 5:15-16)*. It's secret-place wisdom that helps us to know that God has given his angels charge over us, that nothing can touch his child without expressed permission from God to test us **(Psalm 91:11-12).** Secret-place wisdom reminds us to acknowledge God in all our ways so that he will direct our paths **(Proverbs 3:6)**. Never forget no matter how old you are, it is nothing short of a miracle that you have made it this far. Remember, tomorrow isn't promised to any of us. *It is of the Lord's mercies that we are not consumed because his compassions fail not. They are new every morning: great is thy faithfulness. (Lamentations 3:22-23)*

He Will, Keep You From All Danger

Isaiah 26:3 NIV
You will keep in perfect peace those whose minds are steadfast, because they trust in you.

Fear is the paralyzing agent within the enemy's venom. Danger differs from harm in that the threat of injury has not yet come. Before his conversion to the faith, Saul acted similarly under the enemy's influence. While on his way to persecute Christians, the Bible records how Saul breathed out murderous threats to the Lord's followers *(Acts 9:1)*. I'm grateful for God's patience towards Saul, without it, Timothy would have no mentor to encourage him in the knowledge that fear has nothing to do with God, but what God gives equips us to overcome fear every time *(2 Timothy 1:7)*.

Where the spirit of the Lord is, there is liberty. Fear binds us through terrifying pictures of the future. Remember, the enemy is a liar, and God already has a bright future in mind for you *(1 Corinthians 2:9-10)*. So as we walk through the valleys of life, we can have no fear because God is with us. His protection and instruction should comfort us *(Psalm 23:4)*, reminding us that he keeps us from falling.

*Thank the Lord for being a keeper. There is no safer place than in the presence of God, for we are hidden in Christ, safe from all **hurt**, **harm**, and **danger**.*

The name of the Lord is a strong fortress; the godly run to him and are safe. (Proverbs 18:10 NLT)

Heavenly Father, thank you for watching over me. Every hair of mine you've numbered, and every day of my life is written. Help me never to forget that. Insulate me with your presence and shield me from the clamor of the day. The daily news reminds me of the problems we face. Let Your Spirit remind me of the promises You've made. I want to focus on the destiny You have for me, not the uncertainties of the economy. While the world wonders, show me wondrous things from Your word; cause me to rejoice from Your truth more than a man who's found buried treasure.

ELEVEN

A KNOCK AT THE DOOR

REVELATION 3:20

"Behold, I stand at the door, and knock: if any man hear my voice, and open the door, I will come in to him, and will sup with him, and he with me." (Revelation 3:20 KJV)

Jesus said, *"If any man,"* extending his invite to every man and woman, His desire to spend quality time with us. Think of it; God is personally interested in YOU. Such a remarkable thing! It can be hard to fathom this idea! Even the angels are amazed at God's interest in us **(Psalm 8:4-8)**. To some, walking with God and having a personal relationship with the Lord seems so pious and lofty that it is often left to the clergy or super devout. We rob ourselves of great privilege and help when we discount God's knocks as His call for someone else.

Jesus doesn't call out to preachers but to people. How we respond to him will determine how he shapes our lives. I admit the thought of responding to God's call can be scary. In some ways, we are all *"Self-conscience"* to a degree where our focus can be skewed to dwell on how we appear in other people's eyes more than God's. In *Exodus 20:18-21,* Moses pleads with the children of Israel not to be afraid of God's voice. God desired to establish a personal relationship to enable them to live as they should. Instead, the people preferred having Moses as their spiritual spokesman. How common are we likely to do the same? Whether we consider ourselves unworthy, not as spiritual, or not as inclined as others to pray, we leave it to others to speak to God for us. Praying for others is an incredible privilege, but Jesus desires to relate to each of us directly.

Luke 19:5-6 KJV
"And when Jesus came to the place, he looked up, and saw him, and said unto him, Zacchæus, make haste, and come down; for to day I must abide at thy house. And he made haste, and came down, and received him joyfully."

If you think you have to be a *"type of way"* to walk with God, you're mistaken. No home or heart is too "common" for Christ to dwell in. Jesus shattered this notion when he invited himself to Zacchaeus' house. Zacchaeus' profession was tax collector, an attractive role to dishonest and money-hungry people, but seen as a reproachable profession to the broader community. At one point, *"money-hungry"* and *"dishonest"* would have been an accurate description of Zacchaeus' life, but Jesus saw a change in him that others could not; a broken and contrite heart *(Psalm 51:17)*. Over dinner, Zacchaeus confessed to Jesus his journey of repentance, how he'd given to the poor, paid back all he had stolen with interest, and desired to know what he was to do further to align his life to God. While at the table, Jesus confirmed his salvation, validating his genuine heart while expressing God's love for him.

Jesus is not attracted to a particular personality, only sincerity. He knocks at the door, not forcing friendship but desiring it with you and me. We open the door when we open our minds and heart to his voice. We prepare our table to dine with the Lord by preparing a place and time we've set to speak with him. Some people have dedicated setting rooms or prayer corners in their homes as sacred spaces for personal time with the Lord. God honors that, and it's scriptural to do so. Life, however, doesn't always work to our convenience, yet the Lord is available to us at all times and everywhere if we seek Him with our whole hearts. If welcomed, Jesus can come in and commune with us while in the car sitting in a parking lot before a meeting, in the living room as we guide our families, or alone at your desk, strengthening you in your time of need. Wherever you can be honest, Jesus can be present. As we grow in our transparency with the Lord, we grow in our knowledge of Him and His ways *(John 15:15-17)*. Peter was distinguished among the disciples for his leadership, but John was unique to Jesus because of their relationship. Sometimes regarded as *"the one whom Jesus loved" (John 20:2)*, John's Gospel is unique in that he shows us dimensions of Jesus' character we don't see much of in other places. Like John, the goal isn't to see God differently but to know Him intimately. John 1 describes Jesus as the one full of *Grace & Truth*. Anyone who has spent real time with the "gentle redeemer" would not be surprised by Zacchaeus' conversion. At the table, we go from knowing the Lord to being known by Him *(Galatians 4:9)*, cultivating a life-changing relationship.

John 21:12-14 NIV

"Jesus said to them, "Come and have breakfast." None of the disciples dared ask him, "Who are you?" They knew it was the Lord. Jesus came, took the bread and gave it to them, and did the same with the fish. This was now the third time Jesus appeared to his disciples after he was raised from the dead."

Coming to Jesus is necessary for every sinner but doubly important for the saint that believes in Him. Even after knowing He has risen and given us victory, we struggle to draw near to Him to experience His victory. Life's distractions can pull us back into old patterns we once used to self-soothe. Though we know who Jesus is, we grow unsure of ourselves. That is why Jesus doesn't mind knocking. When we shut ourselves up alone with our responsibilities and pressures, Jesus invites us to dine and enjoy the food he's prepared specifically for us. Knowing we are out of answers, He begins the conversation by asking, "Do you love me" **(John 21:15)**? As disciples, let us not neglect our time to dine. Only at the Lord's table can we receive the bread of life *(John 6:35)*, the milk of sincerity *(1Peter 2:2),* the honey of instruction *(Psalm 119:103)*, water from the living well *(John 4:14)*, atoning wine *(Luke 22:20)*, reserved with select meats for strength *(Hebrews 5:14)* and oil for the journey *(Psalm 23:5)*.

"Blessed are they which do hunger and thirst after right-eousness: for they shall be filled."
(Matthew 5:6 KJV)

Lord, allow me to be open to getting to know you better. Allow me to dine with you as a family member without ceremony or formality. Away from the demands of the day and the concerns of tomorrow, I want to be present, right here and now, at the table you have prepared for me. Your knocks of invitation will no longer be ignored now that I know you are calling me away so we may make time to dine in Jesus' name, Amen.

TWELVE

TABLE FOR TWO

PSALM 23:5-6

Thou preparest a table before me in the presence of mine enemies: thou anointest my head with oil; my cup runneth over. Surely goodness and mercy shall follow me all the days of my life: and I will dwell in the house of the Lord forever. (Psalm 23:5-6 KJV)

It's incredible the answers we receive at the table. Even amid adversity, God's intimacy provides peace for the present. His anointing is a healing balm for wounds endured and a reservoir of strength that enables us to continue. Undoubtedly, The Shepard's goodness and mercy are pillars we can depend on despite what life brings our way. Perhaps you can relate; sometimes, we face enormous disappointment, pending pressures, or doubters. Our minds race to dig for answers or the meaning behind our dilemmas. If we took a moment to breathe, we would hear the spirit challenging us to give thanks. 1 Thessalonians 5:18 says, *"In everything give thanks: for this is the will of God in Christ Jesus concerning you."* It's helpful to regard those inner promptings to worship as the Lord's divine invitations to dine serve as our special time for communion.

1 Corinthians 11:23-26 NLT

For I pass on to you what I received from the Lord himself. On the night when he was betrayed, the Lord Jesus took some bread and gave thanks to God for it. Then he broke it in pieces and said, "This is my body, which is given for you. Do this in remembrance of me." In the same way, he took the cup of wine after supper, saying, "This cup is the new covenant between God and his people—an agreement confirmed with my blood. Do this in remembrance of me as often as you drink it." For every time you eat this bread and drink this cup, you are announcing the Lord's death until he comes again.

Jesus gave us communion *(the divine dinner)* to encourage and remind us of what has already been accomplished. The night the savior faced betrayal, pain, and loss, he, too, prepared His table. Why would anyone choose such a time to set a table of communion? Jesus, the Good Shepherd, leads us in the path of life, where his presence brings joy *(Psalm 16:11)*. His joy and peace are distinguished in our difficulties. When we have every reason to be worried, frustrated, or stressed, we are graced with a peculiar calm, patience, and peace. Philippians 4:7 speaks of a *"peace that surpasses all understanding."* Surely our valleys would qualify as a place for little peace. A war zone is the last place anyone would think to host a mid-day meal. Psalms 23 paints a bold picture of peace and refreshment; a dinner table set in the middle of a place most would cry to be rescued. God's amazing grace *(strength)* can be best seen not in His rescue but in His reinforcement. He saves us from trials, while other times, he saves us *"in them."* In the book of Daniel, three friends could have been saved from execution by the fiery furnace. However, God decided to save them *"while IN the furnace."* The three young men were thrown in, bound but soon after were seen walking around, unharmed, and free while talking with Jesus, in no hurry for the door *(Daniel 3:24-27)*. Whatever your furnace may be, God's presence makes the unbearable appear forgettable, not only to those watching from a distance but to us as we look intently at Jesus in the midst of it all.

John 4:10 NLT
Jesus replied, "If you only knew the gift God has for you and who you are speaking to, you would ask me, and I would give you living water."

In Philippians 3:10, Paul passionately expressed his desire to *"Know Him."* Faith and love grow as our knowledge of the person grows. Prayer is highly esteemed but is rarely used for its benefit to us. We sometimes overcomplicate prayer, treating it as an excellent ceremonial practice or a last-resort plea in desperate times. In all sincerity and simplicity, Jesus says, *"Just ask."* Spending time with God isn't meant to be intimidating but intentional and personal. James 4:2 says that *"We have not because we ask not."* The first step to meeting our needs is to meet the Lord at the table of prayer and supplication. Our heavenly father already knows what we need, even before we ask, but we must ask *(Matthew 6:8-13)*.

Full of compassion and love, Jesus told the woman at the well, *"If you only knew who I am,"* you would be asking of me instead of me asking you! God desires to be nearer to us; He's provided a table and urges us to dine. Full of Grace and Truth, Jesus compassionately looks to us, saying, <u>*If you only knew*</u> how I could strengthen and restore you, you would ask me to dine. *"Come to me, all you who are weary and burdened, and I will give you rest. Take my yoke upon you and learn from me, for I am gentle and humble in heart, and you will find rest for your souls. For my yoke is easy, and my burden is light" (Matthew 11:28-30 NIV)*. Our days are busy, and valleys are long; there never seems to be a *"good time"* to dine (pray), so let's exercise our faith through our priorities. Take the time, let's put the world on hold, and commune with the one who holds the world in his hands.

"Did someone bring him food while we were gone?" the disciples asked each other. Then Jesus explained: "My nourishment comes from doing the will of God, who sent me, and from finishing his work. You know the saying, 'Four months between planting and harvest.' But I say, wake up and look around. The fields are already ripe for harvest.
<u>John 4:33-35 NLT</u>

Lord, thank you for hearing me. You always hear me. Though life is noisy, my heart is busy, and my vision is blurred. I'm no longer concerned about the things I don't understand. You are worthy of my praise even if I don't get my way as long as I get YOU. Speak, Lord. Your servant is listening. I don't mind waiting. I've reserved this time for us.

THIRTEEN

A CALL TO UNITY

EPHESIANS 2:13-14

But now you have been united with Christ Jesus. Once you were far away from God, but now you have been brought near to him through the blood of Christ. For Christ himself has brought peace to us. He united Jews and Gentiles into one people when, in his own body on the cross, he broke down the wall of hostility that separated us. (Ephesians 2:13-14 NLT)

Romans 5:1 reveals a beautiful truth; through Christ, we have obtained *"peace with God."* What a statement and timely encouragement! By nature, we were set at odds with God of no original fault of our own - Adam's decision still affects us today. Nevertheless, we were all born with hearts and minds facing away from Him, focused on ourselves. A selfish heart shrinks one's capacity to love or be loved by another person. In such a state, we unknowingly set ourselves at odds with God, all while ignorant of His desire to give us the best of everything. Like a true parent, God's view is long-term, and His intent provides generational benefits *(John 15:16)*. As children, it's hard for us to see "down the road" like dad does while we're looking "at the road," facing daily choices. Overcoming life's choices is experienced when we unite with God's plan. His Spirit gives us the faith to understand *(Hebrews 11:3)* that his plan is best. When we fail to live by faith in God, we are tempted to act against our own best interests.

Romans 8:7 says that the "carnal mind" is hostile toward God; it can not submit to God's will even if it tries. Matthew 16:23-25 gives us an example; Jesus sharply rebukes Peter's disapproval of Jesus having to die. Jesus regarded Peter's words as Satan's advice, explaining that his point of view was short-sighted and concerned only with the things of men instead of God's desires. Like that, we, too, choose what appears easy or helpful and unknowingly affirm that which works contrary to God's perfect plan.

> **<u>1Peter 2:3-5 NLT</u>**
> *"now that you have had a taste of the Lord's kindness. You are coming to Christ, who is the living cornerstone of God's temple. He was rejected by people, but he was chosen by God for great honor. And you are living stones that God is building into his spiritual temple. What's more, you are his holy priests. Through the mediation of Jesus Christ, you offer spiritual sacrifices that please God."*

Ephesians 2:10 says, *"For we are his workmanship, created in Christ Jesus unto good works, which God hath before ordained that we should walk in them."* How incredible is that? To think that each of us is a critical part of God's masterpiece! As exhilarating as that sounds, it's also humbling. God is looking for those who, with willing hearts and hands, will live as His ambassadors to the world **(John 4:23)**. Uniting with God requires our total surrender to his plan and our role in it.

Jesus shared a kingdom parable in **Matthew 13:44** that says, *"The kingdom of heaven is like treasure hidden in a field. When a man found it, he hid it again, and then in his joy went and sold all he had and bought that field."* In part, I equate that scripture to a metaphor of my own; "As the treasure is in the field, so is God's plans in the palm of our hands." We are God's package deal. The truth of God (*to the measure we possess it*) is the treasure of life. On the other hand, we are the field of dirt, made with clay, born to hold it, carry it, and make it accessible to those looking for God's goodness. God desires to be united with us in a way that causes the fruit that His Spirit produces in our character to bless those around us. The life we have in Christ is intended to be full and overflowing. Morning by morning, we are encouraged to go to the Father to receive His daily bread. Unity with God provides a daily restock of grace, which is more intimate than a Sunday Morning worship experience can provide, nor is it meant to replace it. Pray as Jesus taught and watch God supply your personal needs, enabling you to enjoy the strength that only comes by joining other believers in receiving the overflow God reserves for corporate fellowship *(Psalm 133)*.

"For God, who said, "Let there be light in the darkness,"
has made this light shine in our hearts so we could know
the glory of God that is seen in the face of Jesus Christ.
We now have this light shining in our hearts, but we
ourselves are like fragile clay jars containing this great
treasure. This makes it clear that our great power is from
God, not from ourselves."
2 Corinthians 4:6-7 NLT

Lord, I thank you for every person you allow me to encounter. I submit my schedule and agenda to you, trusting that you order the steps of a good man. I won't fret over today's troubles, for they are purposely planned triumphs for Your glory. My prayer is that you guide me in my responses. Help me bless someone's day and not be a stumbling block. I want to reflect Your heart in all that I do. Confirm Your promises, and help me be an answer to someone's prayer today. In Jesus' name, Amen.

FOURTEEN

SONS & DAUGHTERS

JOHN 1:11-13

"He came to that which was his own, but his own did not receive him. Yet to all who did receive him, to those who believed in his name, he gave the right to become children of God— children born not of natural descent, nor of human decision or a husband's will, but born of God." (John 1:11-13 NIV)

What a great thought! God has granted those with whom He had no relationship by His grace alone a sacred status; sons and daughters. To be a son is no honorary title or figure of speech but an accurate description of our place in Him, a literal position. Since *"the fall,"* every human born has an innate desire chiefly turned inward, with a perspective bent towards earthly matters, fixated on physical survival and personal expression. Ephesians 2 teaches we had no *"spiritual life"* before Christ's intervention. We were actually *"dead in trespasses and sins"* **(Ephesians 2:1)** but were made alive (*spiritually*) again with Christ **(Ephesians 2:5)**. God's intentions may have started in Genesis, but Calvary confirmed them. When Christ decided to die, his sacrifice abolished sin's grip over us. The barrier that sin caused between God and us was destroyed forever. For the first time since the Garden of Eden, humanity has been given the power to choose again; life and death. Christ's redeeming work gives us access and the confidence to enter God's presence boldly, just as a prince would entreat their father, the king **(Hebrews. 4:16)**.

John 8:39 NLT
"Our father is Abraham!" they declared. "No," Jesus replied, "for if you were really the children of Abraham, you would follow his example."

In one reply, Jesus summarizes centuries of the scripture while explaining God's heart. Sonship with God is not a matter of flesh but faith. Two opposite errors can occur, which we should pray to avoid. The first is Self-Righteousness. Self-Righteousness is an inward belief that we somehow hold merit with God because of who we are or what we have, independent of Him or anyone else. The Pharisees of Jesus' day linked their righteousness to the natural lineage and cultural connection they shared with Abraham. The same error occurs when someone references their social or family relationship to someone of high esteem to bring credibility to their faith or standing with God. Presumptuously, we say, "I know I'm blessed; my mother is a devout woman of prayer." Thank God for a praying mother, but as my pastor once reminded our church one Sunday morning, *"God doesn't have grandchildren."*

Abraham learned this lesson from God directly. A praying parent can bring about great blessings (Genesis 17:20-21), but God deals with each of us individually. Those who are blessed to have Godly examples as parents are all the more indebted to the Lord for making the gift of faith an inheritable treasure **(2 Timothy 1:5)**. However, as Easu bitterly came to understand, having a faith-filled family is no guarantee of personal salvation **(Hebrews 12:17)**.

On the other hand, Self-loathing is also just as damning to the soul. Often misunderstood as humility, self-loathing devalues one's worth, while humility is an equal appreciation of all things, including oneself. "SELF-loathing," as its name suggests, looks inward and condemns the individual because of personal traits seen as imperfections, be they real or perceived. If one should dwell in this line of thinking for any length of time, it will become easy for a person to develop the belief that they are not worthy of love or help, even from God.

More than anyone, God understands our need to be affirmed, so He frequently reaffirms His unconditional love for us despite our past mistakes or future potential. King David, author of Psalm 23, did not grow up in a palace with perfectly loving, well-adjusted parents; he often received rejection and loneliness at the hands of his earthly father and brothers. Despite his initial station in life, God described David as *"a man after His heart"* **(Acts 13:22)**. It was by faith that David's relationship status with God changed forever. Psalm 2:7 says, *"I will declare the decree: the Lord hath said unto me, Thou art my Son; this day have I begotten thee. (KJV)"*. Sonship was declared to David when he had nothing to offer the Lord but a heart of devotion. God doesn't love us because we are gifted; he has gifted us because He loves us. It's essential to know that God loves unconditionally. Remember, we can never *"live up to God's love,"* but his love empowers us to live out our destiny. Living out his plan pleases Him greatly. It's encouraging to know that we can make God smile simply by walking His path for us. There is no better portrait of this fact than Jesus. At his baptism and before he had performed a single miracle, his relationship to the Father was already declared and established; "And a voice from heaven said, *"This is my Son, whom I love; with him, I am well pleased."* **(Mathew 3:17 NIV).**

> **Galatians 3:26-29 NIV**
> *"So in Christ Jesus you are all children of God through faith, for all of you who were baptized into Christ have clothed yourselves with Christ. There is neither Jew nor Gentile, neither slave nor free, nor is there male and female, for you are all one in Christ Jesus. If you belong to Christ, then you are Abraham's seed, and heirs according to the promise."*

May the Lord guard your heart against shame, rejection, doubt, and despair. You are His, and HE is your Father. We are often tempted in complex trials to doubt His presence, love, and intentions toward us. We tend to take our gaze away from Him and focus on ourselves. But all who are in Christ is a new creation, the old is passed away, and all as become new **(2 Corinthians 5:17)**. Imagine the victories we would experience in succession if we were to rehearse the promise of 2 Corinthians 5:17 every morning! When we only see ourselves amid trouble, we are overwhelmed by our powerlessness to change the circumstances. Our lack of personal righteousness cannot demand the justice we seek during mistreatments, so our hope suffers assault by the thoughts of past mistakes.

Mistakes will happen as we *"grow along"* this walk, as some are necessary for growth. Wisdom is not shown in how much you know but in how well you learn. Being wise does not mean you are perfect, but you welcome the instruction to improve yourself. In part, Proverbs 9:8 says that whoever *"rebukes a wise man"* will gain *"the wise man's"* love. While still young, no child thanks their parents for the correction they receive; but they are mature by it.

In times of correction, love and trust for the Father sustain us until understanding arrives. Eventually, as we mature, we understand Godly discipline's purpose.

Hebrews 12:6-11 NLT

"For the Lord disciplines those he loves, and he punishes each one he accepts as his child." As you endure this divine discipline, remember that God is treating you as his own children. Who ever heard of a child who is never disciplined by its father? If God doesn't discipline you as he does all of his children, it means that you are illegitimate and are not really his children at all. Since we respected our earthly fathers who disciplined us, shouldn't we submit even more to the discipline of the Father of our spirits, and

live forever? For our earthly fathers disciplined us for a few years, doing the best they knew how. But God's discipline is always good for us, so that we might share in his holiness. 11 No discipline is enjoyable while it is happening—it's painful! But afterward there will be a peaceful harvest of right living for those who are trained in this way."

"See what great love the Father has lavished on us, that we should be called children of God! And that is what we are! The reason the world does not know us is that it did not know him. Dear friends, now we are children of God, and what we will be has not yet been made known. But we know that when Christ appears, we shall be like him, for we shall see him as he is."
1 John 3:1-2 NIV

Heavenly Father, help me understand what it means to be more like you. Some days I am overjoyed by the work you have done in my life, and I'm encouraged by the growth. On other days, I feel unworthy to be called your child, but I am thankful that your Righteousness makes me acceptable. By faith, I ask that you continue to grant me the heritage of those that love you. Dad... I need you if I am going to be who I have been born to become. Thank you for accepting me and counting me as your beloved. In Jesus' name, Amen.

FIFTEEN

LORD, IF YOU SAY SO

MATTHEW 14:27-29

But Jesus immediately said to them: "Take courage! It is I. Don't be afraid." "Lord, if it's you," Peter replied, "tell me to come to you on the water." "Come," he said. Then Peter got down out of the boat, walked on the water and came toward Jesus. (Matthew 14:27-29 NIV)

Be careful what you pray for; you may get it. Life in Christ is a journey of ever-increasing steps in faith. The challenges of yesteryear seem laughable when compared to today's mountains. Be encouraged by the fact that we overcame past impossibilities with Christ's help and that He stands with us today, guiding and cheering us on as we take another set of *"first steps"* toward a new level of faith. Romans 1:17 reminds us that God's plan for complete salvation is comprehensive and progressive. The New Living Translation says, *"This Good News tells us how God makes us right in his sight. This is accomplished from start to finish by faith. As the Scriptures say, "It is through faith that a righteous person has life."*

God is an understanding father who knows the best way to grow us; through stages. At this point in Matthew 14, Peter had an established concept of who

Jesus was, like many of us. He and the disciples knew Him as a healer, feeder of thousands, and forgiver of sins. Until now, Peter and the others in the boat have not yet known Jesus as *"the enabler."* Just as He promised, His Spirit works through us today, enabling us to do, endure, accomplish, and understand what is impossible for us alone *(Ephesians 3:16-20).* So as we continue to walk by faith, We are challenged step by step to trust Him.

Psalm 18:35-36 KJV
"Thou hast also given me the shield of thy salvation: and thy right hand hath holden me up, and thy gentleness hath made me great. Thou hast enlarged my steps under me, that my feet did not slip."

Matthew 14 further reveals an exciting experience and observation. The disciples saw Peter impressively walk on water, but Peter saw Jesus! When Peter took his sights off of Jesus, he sank as his miraculous walk faded from view. When God's peace, strength, and love are at work within us, we can inspire those around us too. To do so, we must follow Peter's lead but desperately cling to God to stay afloat in order to walk over our stormy waves. When we receive the grace to follow Jesus, others are inspired to believe and do the same. Through your act of faith, God accomplishes multiple miracles while maturing one believer; He builds the faith of others! Those who watch, witness God's glory, while those who walk, experience His grace. God performs this miracle every day and gives us the opportunity to play a part at any moment. God purposely accomplishes the miraculous through our lives without separating us from the human experience.

2 Corinthians 4:6-7 NLT
"For God, who said, "Let there be light in the darkness," has made this light shine in our hearts so we could know

the glory of God that is seen in the face of Jesus Christ. We
now have this light shining in our hearts, but we ourselves
are like fragile clay jars containing this great treasure.
This makes it clear that our great power is from God, not
from ourselves."

Jesus said, *"In the same way, let your good deeds shine out for all to see so that*
everyone will praise your heavenly Father" (**Matthew 5:16 NLT**). We *"walk on*
water" every day we open our eyes. It doesn't always feel that way; God's grace
is so faithful it often goes undetected as we take care of the mundane tasks of
the day. Whether we "feel" His presence or not, we bring our best effort daily,
trusting Him moment by moment, leaving the results to God. Trusting Jesus'
invitation *"to come"* is what Peter did to spark this miraculous moment. His feet
felt no "special sensation" while walking on water, but the scriptures plainly say
he walked. The same is the case with us; when we've done all we can to stand,
we continue to stand and believe that the Lord keeps us up, especially when
we don't *feel* Him. The Lord keeps us completely self-aware of our weaknesses
while abundantly showering us with His grace. Difficulties will surely come,
but humble awareness of our need for the Lord's strength gives us access to His
unlimited supply. The impossible becomes possible for those who believe, and
the mundane becomes miraculous when connected to the Father.

Finally, take note of Jesus' first words to Peter, *"take courage."* How necessary
is that statement for those who desire to live a life worthy of God's call? Take
courage; God has a plan for us with a far greater end than we can imagine. To
get us to our desired destination, He leads us by His word through unfamiliar
terrain, making our belief in Him critical and our experience with Him tangible.
Remember that not all miracles are instantaneous; some manifest through a series of intentional moments that bring about undeniable change. We are God's
handiwork, miracles in the making, but our patience will ultimately prove His
good, perfect, and acceptable will for our lives (**Romans 12:2**). Amid trouble,
even to the point of disaster, Jesus tells His disciples in Luke 21:19, *"In your pa-*

tience possess ye your souls" (KJV). The New Living Translation says, *"By standing firm, you will win your souls."* So again, take courage, for even though the miracle of salvation is received in a moment by belief, it will take a lifetime of patience and continuous devotion to experience it fully. 2 Corinthians 3:18 describes this ever-increasing experience when it says, *"And we all, who with unveiled faces contemplate the Lord's glory, are being transformed into his image with ever-increasing glory, which comes from the Lord, who is the Spirit"* (NIV). While on this journey, our changes occur even when we feel like slipping and battling doubt. Jesus has bid us *to walk to Him*; as we do so, the world will witness yet another disciple's walk on water.

"Now unto him that is able to keep you from falling, and to present you faultless before the presence of his glory with exceeding joy, To the only wise God our Saviour, be glory and majesty, dominion and power, both now and ever. Amen."
Jude 24-25 KJV

Father, I believe that with You, all things are possible. Today, I need your word to confirm my desires. The odds are against me, and there is no guarantee that I can pull this off outside of you. Despite the many reasons I may fear, I stand ready to respond to your permission. If you say, go, help me to go forth boldly. If you say no, give me the grace to wait on You patiently. In Jesus' name, Amen.

SIXTEEN

FIGHTING DOUBT

MATTHEW 14:29-31

So He said, "Come." And when Peter had come down out of the boat, he walked on the water to go to Jesus. But when he saw that the wind was boisterous, he was afraid; and beginning to sink he cried out, saying, "Lord, save me!" And immediately Jesus stretched out His hand and caught him, and said to him, "O you of little faith, why did you doubt?" (Matthew 14:29-31 NKJV)

Despite present accomplishments or past triumphs, doubt can settle in whenever our focus shifts to the wrong things. With Peter's gaze fixed on Jesus, he walked on water like dry ground but soon lost footing after seeing the winds and waves. How easily can we forget God's promises when we traverse unfamiliar territory? Whether a new job, new opportunity, added responsibility, or an incredible unique privilege, doubt can cause us to forget that God has called us to a life worthy of the call we have received *(Ephesians 4:1)*. Popular psychology has coined the phrase *"imposter syndrome."* In his 2008 Harvard Business Review article, <u>Overcoming Imposter Syndrome</u>[1] , Gill Corkindale defined it *"as a collection of feelings of inadequacy that persist despite evident success. 'Imposters' suffer from chronic self-doubt and a sense of intellectual fraudulence that override any feelings of success or external proof of their competence."*

Doubt is an enemy we all battle, whether fretting over tomorrow's forecast or questioning yesterday's choices. I've learned to find comfort in knowing that our daily occasions never catch God off guard. As Jesus reaches out to save Peter, He inquires about the existence of Peter's doubt. As far as Jesus was concerned (walking on water himself), Peter had no valid reason to panic. As incredible as this may sound, the same is the case for us; God allows times of significant testing to be turned to triumph through our faith in Him. The secret to our *"secure footing"* is found in our continual focus. Jesus asks Peter, Why did you doubt? Jesus could have said, *Peter, why did you look away?* Today the Spirit of Christ urges us to consider how we would answer the same question. How easy is it to look away? When problems arise, we may call out for help, but only after our focus has turned away from what holds us to that which threatens us. The threat of danger isn't the only thing that can bring on sinking; the unexpected waves of good fortune are notorious attention grabbers. A moment of indulgence could quickly become a season of fruitless inactivity. No one intends to make missteps, but stumbling is inevitable when we forfeit our focus.

Hebrews 12:1-3: MSG

"Do you see what this means—all these pioneers who blazed the way, all these veterans cheering us on? It means we'd better get on with it. Strip down, start running—and never quit! No extra spiritual fat, no parasitic sins. Keep your eyes on Jesus, who both began and finished this race we're in. Study how he did it. Because he

---

1. https://hbr.org/2008/05/overcoming-imposter-syndrome

never lost sight of where he was headed—that exhilarating finish in and with God—he could put up with anything along the way: Cross, shame, whatever. And now he's there, in the place of honor, right alongside God. When you find yourselves flagging in your faith, go over that story again, item by item, that long litany of hostility he plowed through. That will shoot adrenaline into your souls!"

As a young man, my late pastor and mentor, Bishop C.L. Long, often said, _"Keep focused and keep moving."_ If you feel you've made a misstep here or there, dust yourself off and get back at it. It's hard to tell when you're in the thickest adversity, but a tremendous transformation is taking place. One thing is for sure; God cares more about how we're doing in the storm than the storm itself. After all, He's God; there's no challenge for Him to quiet a storm when He prefers to calm a soul to trust Him. Raging waves are child's play to God; His glory is found in our rising level of faith. It is a more remarkable act of God to change a human heart than it is for Him to change the weather. Feelings of doubt and inadequacies depend on us "not" depending on God. Self-reliance, while on the surface having admirable qualities, has a side effect that makes "living by faith" unbearably tricky. Strictly living "by sight," as the scripture describes, causes anxiety which can produce a cynical and desperate worldview *(Matthew 6:25-34, 1 Corinthians 2:13-14)*. Trusting in the Lord is believing beyond the possibilities of personal capability.

Doubt can either make us freeze for fear or frantically drive us to overreact. I applaud Peter's faithful beginning as he walked to Jesus, but I can personally identify with his eventual flailing and splashing with cries for help. Doubt causes us to lose sight of the support that has always been there by shifting our focus to a new stimulus or a sudden challenge. When we lose sight of who's holding us up, we lose faith that we can stand; this hurls us from peace into a panic. Refrain from misunderstanding; genuine faith requires action *(James 2:14-17)*, but in testing times, the action most needed is resting! *Hebrews 4:9-11* illustrates this beautifully.

"There remaineth therefore a rest to the people of God. For he that is entered into his rest, he also hath ceased from his own works, as God did from his. Let us labour therefore to enter into that rest, lest any man fall after the same example of unbelief." (KJV)

We will continually learn the areas where we must work on being "totally dependent" on God. In some areas, we excel in trusting God. While in other categories, there is room for improvement as we continually need to improve. Prayer becomes our biggest weapon in employing God's help to understand better the weight that hinders us. God goes one step further to reveal the scenarios that often sway our hearts and minds to distrust, impulsivity, and overreaction. In the last words of verse 11, we see the cause; unbelief! Rest (peace) is a benefit we receive because of faith in God. Sin (to fall short) produces stress as an adverse effect of "unbelief"! Let this be an encouragement and a reminder never to stop believing that you can do "ALL things" through Christ who strengthens you *(Philippians 4:13).*

<u>**Psalms 46:1-3 NKJV**</u>
"God is our refuge and strength, A very present help in trouble. Therefore we will not fear, Even though the earth be removed, And though the mountains be carried into the [b]midst of the sea; Though its waters roar and be troubled, Though the mountains shake with its swelling. Selah"

Selah - Take a moment, listen, and consider the belief found in Psalm 46:1-3 and how much it is expressed through unimaginable peace. Take this time to trade your doubts for God's assurance *(1Peter 5:7)*

And when the disciples saw it, they marveled, saying, "How did the fig tree wither away so soon?" So Jesus answered and said to them, "Assuredly, I say to you, if you have faith and do not doubt, you will not only do what was done to the fig tree, but also if you say to this mountain, 'Be removed and be cast into the sea,' it will be done. 22 And whatever things you ask in prayer, believing, you will receive."
<u>Matthew 21:20-22 NKJV</u>

Lord, I Believe! But.....Help my unbelief. In Jesus' name, Amen.

SEVENTEEN

ALL THINGS MADE NEW

PSALM 32:1-2

"Blessed is he whose transgression is forgiven, whose sin is covered. Blessed is the man unto whom the Lord imputeth not iniquity, and in whose spirit there is no guile." (Psalm 32:1-2 KJV)

1 John 1:8 says, *"If we say that we have no sin, we deceive ourselves, and the truth is not in us."* The truth is, we have all fallen short, whether in thought, deed, or word. As we confront our limitations, it's common to respond with the phrase, *"I am only human."* We do not measure our faith by our perfection but by the perfecting process **(Philippians 3:12-14)**. The gradual growth we endure daily is found most when honesty meets reality. 1 John 1:9 continues, *"If we confess our sins, he is faithful and just to forgive us our sins, and to cleanse us from all unrighteousness."* What an incredible promise! To know that you have a faithful advocate who is there for the good and regretful times. Knowing this, Hebrews 4:16 encourages us all to come boldly to the throne of grace, where we will find help in the time of need. There is no greater time of need than when we realize our need for a savior.

There aren't many verses more humbling than the one declared in Psalm 103:14; "*God knows our frame.*" He knows what we are capable of, what we can handle, and, more importantly, what we cannot. That is what makes the Gospel such an expression of love and wisdom. Romans 5:6 says, "*When we were utterly helpless, Christ came at just the right time and died for us, sinners.*" We are powerless to correct past mistakes; that powerlessness brings regrets today and fearful thoughts of the future. In our best moments, we are powerless against sin and the regret it causes, but thank God; in His strength, we are victorious. Be encouraged, and rest assured that Christ can lift and cure every burden of the soul.

Matthew 19:25-26 NLT
The disciples were astounded. "Then who in the world can be saved?" they asked. Jesus looked at them intently and said, "Humanly speaking, it is impossible. But with God everything is possible."

What a reason to rejoice! There is no longer a *"guilty verdict"* or *"sentence of punishment"* for those who live by faith in Christ Jesus. We are free to live on an everlasting path that leads to life instead of one plagued by dead-end decisions **(Romans 8:1-2)**! A promise this awesome can sometimes be hard to imagine, especially when fighting feelings of regret and pain. Remember, there is a fine line between conviction and condemnation. To be convicted is to "*be made to see*" the full implications of your ways. Condemned is *reserved for punishment* without an opportunity to correct errors and no hope for reconsidering the judgment received. While both involve pain, conviction is the ***prick*** our hearts need to encourage change. At the same time, condemnation is the ***thrusting pierce*** of an enemy's spear to destroy *(2 Corinthians 7:10)*. When it comes to the pricks of conviction, be encouraged by this discomfort. It's reassurance that the shepherd's voice is still precious to you *(John 10:27)*. All that is left is the proper response. Hebrews 3:15 says, "*If you hear his voice today, don't* *be stubborn like those who rebelled."* I empathize with anyone recovering from recent failures and battling regret; moving forward is hard, especially when you question your judgment. It is unpleasant when we make mistakes; it can be discouraging and disappointing. Our first impulse is to stop the pain and the regret it's causing. Not to mention, personal revelation can sometimes be brutal to come to terms with. It's as if we would prefer to have our senses numbed rather than confront the realities of our actions face to face. The desire to avoid conviction's pain is the hard-heartedness *Hebrews 3:15* pleads with us to resist. Maintaining a heart that is receptive to God's voice is central to our relationship with him and is the single ingredient God uses to transform and deliver us in times of need.

Matthew 9:5 KJV
"For whether is easier, to say, Thy sins be forgiven thee; or to say, Arise, and walk?"

Sin is the problem, be it a crippling condition or a clouded conscience. Sin paralyzes destiny's potential, whether by indirect consequence or crippling the conscience towards good works. Though we may know the good we should do, sin robs us of our boldness to act by plaguing our minds with past regrets. In Mark 9:5, we see Jesus heal a paralytic while healing the perspectives of those around him and those who would later hear of this miracle. Jesus asked the crowd which phrase would make them feel better about receiving the same outcome. God's message of forgiveness can be summed up in a simple command; *"get up, and get moving."* When God forgives, he separates us from our sin as far as the East is from the West *(Psalm 103:12)*, never to be brought up again. Removing such a weight invigorates us with new life and strength, justifying us to stand with further assurance, confidence, peace, and stability. Which is easiest for you to hear today? God extends to us now both a pardon for the past and permission for our future. *You are forgiven!*

"This then is the message which we have heard of him, and declare unto you, that God is light, and in him is no darkness at all. but if we walk in the light, as he is in the light, we have fellowship one with another, and the blood of Jesus Christ his Son cleanseth us from all sin."
__1 John 1:5, 7 KJV__

Father, I thank you that the blood of Jesus cleanses me from my sins. At times I wrestle with the memories of my past. By faith, I accept your forgiveness and the healing it provides, granting me a clear conscience. I surrender my mistakes and reputation to You, trusting You to care for them both, knowing that You can work everything out for my good. In Jesus' name, Amen.

EIGHTEEN

NEW CREATURE, NEW DIRECTION

2 CORINTHIANS 5:17

"Therefore if any man be in Christ, he is a new creature: old things are passed away; behold, all things are become new." (2 Corinthians 5:17 KJV)

God is the excellent slate cleaner! If any person is "In Christ," he is a new creation. The clean slate that God provides is no mere "second chance" or "do-over," but God creates "again" a completely remade person with new hope and a future. So what does "In Christ" really mean? Perhaps only a lifetime of walking in this blessed reality will enable us to appreciate and experience this privilege's impact fully. I grew to learn, however, that this privilege is as conditional as it is fantastic. Not to be confused with God's love, which is unconditional **(John 3:16)**, God's blessings come in response to having a "right relationship" with Him. Only "In Christ" do we experience His Yes and Amen **(2 Corinthians 1:20)**.

Apart from God, we can only hope to receive His mercy. Though God is rich in mercy, we rob ourselves of the privilege that brings righteousness, joy, and peace when we seek to build our lives outside of his borders **(Romans 14:17)**. Jesus encourages us to "abide" in Him as He is the true vine; the life source from which we find the strength to grow, produce fruit, and flourish. Being "in Christ" is displayed through a life transformed, first in the heart, then indeed. "In Christ" means being dependent on and identified by Christ through our lives. Abiding in God permits God to extend his grace to us as a father responds to his beloved children **(Ephesians 1:6)**.

Romans 8:1-2 NLT
"So now there is no condemnation for those who belong to Christ Jesus. And because you belong to him, the power of the life-giving Spirit has freed you from the power of sin that leads to death."

Remember what Romans 8 teaches. You are a child of God if the Spirit of Christ dwells in you. His life-giving Spirit empowers us for a life of freedom. Christ empowers us to live free from daily life's imminent fears and fortunes. These daily impulses seek to lead us into a scarcity mindset, making us susceptible to our whims, anxieties, presumptions, and selfish desires. We grow in God's freedom as our understanding of our relationship with Him grows. As His children, we have an inheritance, shared with Christ **(Romans 8:17)**, that is incorruptible - impossible to spoil and promised to last forever! Such promises cover us in the security of knowing just how special we are to God.

No matter how seasoned in faith we are, everyone struggles occasionally with our adoption. We may question how someone with our past or current struggles can consider ourselves a "child of God." Remember, Christ settled that matter at the cross, and though the enemy will still flood your mind with thoughts of unworthiness, be encouraged and secure in the fact that the Lord knows who belongs to Him. He decided to die for you before you knew who He was. Let the gospel *(good news)* of God settle you. Knowing who you are to Him means everything; it impacts how we live our lives. Because of Christ, we have peace with God **(Romans 5:1)**, so remain "in Christ" so His peace will comfort you from your past and give you hope for the future.

We have great hope for the future because of the power of His life-giving Spirit. Remember, there is **no condemnation with God** because, without Him, we were condemned already **(John 3:17)**. Condemning thoughts are from the *evil one* and very different from the thoughts of conviction the Holy Spirit uses to bring about change. To be convicted means to be "made to see." To be convicted of God's love is to see it for what it truly is, unconditional. God's love ignites in us a new heart with godly desires. His love provokes us to want to do better, not by obligation but as an offering of love, just as He did for us on Calvary. Such a change in heart can not be brought about by rules and regulations but by love and relationship. As God seeks to build a relationship with us, we become more aware of the areas in our lives that are being transformed to please Him. As we give ourselves to the Lord's purpose, we desire Him more, and His will becomes our will until our lives externally reflect the inner workings He had begun in our hearts. Amid this miraculous transformation, we fight satan's effort to discourage us by kicking up the dust of past mistakes, magnifying them with the rules, regulations, and religious platitudes we've failed to exemplify. He does this to flood us with feelings of unworthiness and shame. However, we must never forget that Christ has made all things new. Our only debt is to the present moment and how we are to please the Lord. Remember that the cross of Christ provides mercy for our past and grace for our future.

2 Corinthians 5:16-17 NLT

"So we have stopped evaluating others from a human point of view. At one time we thought of Christ merely from a human point of view. How differently we know him now! This means that anyone who belongs to Christ has become a new person. The old life is gone; a new life has begun!"

Discouragement draws its power from our dependence on our strength. When we look for the more abundant life God promises from a human perspective, we unknowingly discount the supernatural work responsible for the change. We sell ourselves short by not trusting God to "be God." He is the only one who can completely transform the human heart. In so doing, God cuts at "the heart" of everything concerning us, revealing our true intentions, strengths, and weakness **(Hebrews 4:12)**. God goes beyond the surface level to the root of our will, perfecting the motives behind our actions. Our lives can only reflect our capacity to love and understand others. Faithfulness in any relationship is a fruit of love and commitment. To increase his faithfulness, the psalmist asked God to "enlarge his heart" to love Him more, which would enable him to continue to walk in the ways of the Lord **(Psalms 119:32)**. The key to our walking in victory with the Lord; is maintaining our relationship with Him.

God not only gives us a clean slate for the past, but He sets us up for success by giving us a new grace for our future. True repentance occurs as we grow closer to seeing matters the way God sees them. Our love for Him enables us to align our lives to match the calling we have in Him. Without a relationship, we are left with a mere outward regiment. So let us not be weary in well doing; keep pressing to know God better. God blesses our perseverance with a grace that will produce a hope that will never disappoint **(Romans 5:4-5)**. The more we yield to His direction, the more God reveals his purpose for us. As we submit to Jesus, the author and perfector of our faith, we experience a progressive transformation that fulfills a promise God made in Ezekiel 36:26-27 NLT: *"And I will give you a new heart, and I will put a new spirit in you. I will take out your stony, stubborn heart and give you a tender, responsive heart. And I will put my Spirit in you so that you will follow my decrees and be careful to obey my regulations."*

Ephesians 4:22-24 KJV
"That ye put off concerning the former conversation the old man, which is corrupt according to the deceitful lusts;

**And be renewed in the spirit of your mind; And that
ye put on the new man, which after God is created in
righteousness and true holiness."**

Do you ever wonder how God makes this "new direction" possible? He does so
by giving us new desires. Since we have been *made brand new*, we must embrace
the new life He has imparted to us. To *"put off the former conversation of the
old man"* means to abandon the priorities that drove us before becoming aware
of God's plan. Now that we have a relationship with God, we gain access to
better promises and the power to live in a way that pleases God, not to *appease*
Him. We mustn't mistake God's grace as a license to do what we please, but
to accomplish our purpose *(Romans 6:1-2)*. God's grace doesn't make our
wrongs right; instead, it is the power of God to help us understand and do
what is right according to God's will. A word of caution here as many have
mishandled the mercy and grace of God. Though God abounds in grace and
love, we must be careful in handling the richness of His mercy. Just as we would
receive a charitable gift from a Billionaire with scores of disposable income, we
do not discount his gift because of how little it takes away from his net worth.
We receive his gift graciously because of how much it changes our lives. With
the same spirit of gratitude, let us seek the grace of God to live as we should and
not use it frivolously. Because of the richness of his love, the debt of our past has
been paid, and the road to our destiny has been paved. God has made all things
new!

"Christ suffered for our sins once for all time. He never sinned, but he died for sinners to bring you safely home to God. He suffered physical death, but he was raised to life in the Spirit. So he went and preached to the spirits in prison— those who disobeyed God long ago when God waited patiently while Noah was building his boat. Only eight people were saved from drowning in that terrible flood. And that water is a picture of baptism, which now saves you, not by removing dirt from your body, but as a response to God from a clean conscience. It is effective because of the resurrection of Jesus Christ."
1 Peter 3:18-21 NLT

Father, I thank You for the change Your Spirit has made in me. Because of you, I see and desire what you want for me, and I am overwhelmed. You have given me victory over fear and the lies of the past. I am who You say that I am. A child of God, Your child, created for Your purpose. Keep me forever in your care, in Jesus' name, Amen.

NINETEEN

FAMILIAR FOES

LUKE 4:13

When the devil had finished all this tempting, he left him until an opportune time. (Luke 4:13 NIV)

As we recently explored, there is no greater joy than one who has been restored **(Psalm 32)**. With the cleansing power of God, we have been equipped for the days ahead and graced for the decisions that will shape our future. Many of these decisions will involve confrontations initiated by the enemy of our soul; *"But thanks be to God, who gives us the victory through our Lord Jesus Christ"* **(1 Corinthians 15:57)**; our future is secure.

Whether recently delivered from temptation or triumphantly standing over them, Christ's encounter in the desert reveals a pattern in the enemy's tactics that we should not ignore. For what satan lacks in control over us, he works to compensate with persistence and subtlety *(Acts 13:10)*. No matter how many victories we experience over trials; we will never be without the pressure of testing. On the subject of life and difficulty, an elder told me: *"Son... keep on living. If you're not in a trial now, you're either coming out of one or on your way there."* Such statements are not meant to discourage us but serve as sayings to remind us of life's *"cyclical nature"* and the necessity of readiness. In Luke 4:13, we see Jesus victorious over temptation, while at the same time, satan looks ahead to another day in hopes of a more *"opportune"* time to yield evil results. The case is the same for us; as we navigate the present-day temptations, we find them fueled by the same old tricks.

2 Corinthians 2:11 NIV
"in order that Satan might not outwit us. For we are not unaware of his schemes."

On the subject of temptation and spiritual warfare, C.S. Lewis once wrote, *"There are two equal and opposite errors into which our race can fall about the devils. One is to disbelieve in their existence. The other is to believe, and to feel an excessive and unhealthy interest in them."*[1] Lewis' acute observation merits reflection. In one area or another, we are not immune to becoming off-balanced in faith or life focus. Sometimes we throw ourselves into work and depend on others to pray for us, perhaps because we fear being regarded as "too spiritual" or disconnected from the day-to-day realities. Others find a way to attribute every undesirable life occurrence in part or whole to unseen forces at work against them. As it is with everything, guarding against the error of exaggeration in any direction is a must. Success for us is found by clinging tightly to the guardrails of scripture. On the subject of satan especially, *1 Peter 5:8* encourages us with these words:

"Be sober, be vigilant; because your adversary the devil, as a roaring lion, walketh about, seeking whom he may devour:" KJV *(emphasis added)*

Never forget and be encouraged that satan has been defeated *(Colossians*

---

1. Preface to the Screwtape Letters. Copyright 1961, restored 1996 C.S. Lewis Pte. Ltd.

2:13-15), making our walk in victory largely dependent on our choices. Being sober means being self-aware and under control. Vigilance is constantly watching, ever attentive and ready. Peter points out this ever-present tension we will face as long as we live. Every new goal and every opportunity for growth is not without its times of adversity and quagmires. In every cycle of struggle, there is a pattern for safe passage. Ecclesiastes 1:9 says, *"The thing that hath been, it is that which shall be; and that which is done is that which shall be done: and there is no new thing under the sun."* (KJV)

"Under the sun," Ecclesiastes is an observational commentary of the cyclical phenomenon we call "life on earth." While we have new life in Christ (spiritual), life on earth has repeatable seasons. As sure as winter follows autumn, the author of our trials and temptations works to gain advantage through the subtly of perceivable patterns we repeat in our affections and behavior. As it is written, *"There is nothing new under the sun,"* so there's a strong chance that our next test will greatly resemble our last, if not in another form. 1 John 2:16 says that all "the world" can offer us are the same three things; the lust of the flesh (physical delights and desire), the lust of the eye (what we can obtain), and the pride of life (how we are seen or admired by others). These subtle blindsides are central to our regretful decisions, impulses, or self-defeating behavior.

I often think about Peter's moment walking on water. He was successful as long as he kept his eyes on Jesus. There are moments when we soar above our challenges while meeting high demands and encouraging others. Our success comes when we focus on being a blessing instead of looking for one. In our best moments, we hardly notice what we are doing. We are too consumed with purpose, love, and passion. We are oblivious to how we appear to "walk on water" to those around us. Other times, a familiar foe called "comparison" *(pride of life)* comes to mind and turns our gaze away from purpose to our peers. The comparison paints an unfair picture leading us to place skewed value on what

---

1. Preface to the Screwtape Letters. Copyright 1961, restored 1996 C.S. Lewis Pte. Ltd.

we are meant to do in light of others with unique skill sets and callings. Left to a biased point of view, we will either appear superior or grossly inferior to the peers we're mentally sizing up. God saves us from this pain by declaring his perfect plan for each of us *(Jeremiah 29:11, Psalms 139:16)*. To be secure in such promises, we must continuously look to Him. We are saved and changed as we continue to behold HIM *(2 Corinthians 3:18)*. These three imposters of happiness *(1 John 2:16)* seek to rob us of our joy by taking advantage of the changing seasons of our lives. For this cause, we must be aware of the pattern. For instance, we may be most vulnerable to thoughts of "comparison" while enjoying moments of personal accomplishment or recovering from seasons of setbacks. What are some of your temptation triggers? It's to your advantage that you know what they are.

When emotions are high (for better or worse), discernment can run low. We become less aware of the needs of others and develop a skewed self-view. Our view of self or life's circumstances is never more out of sync than when we compare it to the conditions of others. Only two extremes can result; inflated self-worth or self-condemnation. Described as a roaring lion walking about, our enemy hungers for our demise, which *he alone can not make possible without our help*. In the hunt for our soul, the enemy wants to use "perfect timing." How aware are you of the times you are most vulnerable to temptation? The enemy intentionally brings ill to God's will for us, but he can do nothing unless we give him space to do so *(Ephesians 4:27)*. As the enemy prowls, we must pray, ensuring that only we take advantage of *the pattern*.

James 1:13-14 NLT

"And remember, when you are being tempted, do not say, "God is tempting me." God is never tempted to do wrong, and he never tempts anyone else. Temptation comes from our own desires, which entice us and drag us away."

As 2 Corinthians 2:11 guards us against staying ignorant of our enemy, James 1:13 helps reminds us not to ignore our vices. After all, how can we successfully defend our position if we need clarity on where we stand? Remember Peter's advice; be sober. Putting it bluntly, the devil doesn't make us do anything. Some of our most regrettable moments came from acts of our own volition. We wanted to say or do what we did, even if we now wish we could take it back. We've discovered that the enemy needs time to *"trick us"* into doing wrong.

On the other hand, impulsive reactions or outbursts say more about our inner desires than the enemy's schemes *(Galatians 5:19-21)*. For instance, long-harbored offenses and contrary desires are ticking time bombs of our own making that threaten our destiny *(Proverbs 4:23)*. In the *KJV Bible, James 1:14* uses the word *"lust"* instead of *"desires."* I believe "lust" is a more accurate translation, although nowadays, lust is often heard with religious overtones concerning sexual immorality. Lust means "strong desire." After all, that is what temptation is; it pulls and lures our attention to immediate satisfaction while closing our eyes to long-term implications. This seduction can happen to us in any area of life, be it career choices or cake slices. Of course, our ignorance of these minor intrusions is quickly dismissed and otherwise justified by noble intentions, making us vulnerable to their threat to our stability. Be encouraged, you are not alone in your struggle, and as odd as things may seem, you are not the first to have encountered the challenges you face. 1 Corinthians 10:13 NIV says, *"No temptation has overtaken you except what is common to mankind. And God is faithful; he will not let you be tempted beyond what you can bear. But when you are tempted, he will also provide a way out so that you can endure it".*

Hebrews 12:1 NLT

"Therefore, since we are surrounded by such a huge crowd of witnesses to the life of faith, let us strip off every weight that slows us down, especially the sin that so easily trips us up. And let us run with endurance the race God has set before us."

God speaks directly to us, poignantly and privately, when necessary. The scriptures serve as a mirror. God's word helps us see ourselves better as we look intently into them. One of the blessings of Hebrews 12:1 is to help us be transparent and honest with ourselves. God understands our imperfections but desires us to deal directly with the gory details. Any one of us can begin with the laundry list of thoughts we've had before lunchtime! Jesus gave insight into this when he noted that *"the way that leads to destruction is broad"* **(Matthew 7:13)** and that few people will find the narrow gate that leads to life. The challenge is choice. If given any law or rule to abide by, the human heart will find ten loopholes to get what it wants without breaking the law. That may be why Hebrews 12:1 does not bother to name any particular sins. Instead, the scriptures cut to the quick and ask us to narrow in on *"the sin."* No matter what the sin may be, it is clear that everyone has one, but God is gracious in inviting us to deal with Him directly in such cases. After all, only God can change the human heart.

If we confess our sins, he is faithful and just and will forgive us our sins and purify us from all unrighteousness. 1 John 1:9 NIV

Some battles are best won when we learn how to run. Remember, the temptation is not a temptation unless it is, in part, a desire of ours. Whether motivated by anger to avenge a wrong or the passion for possessing a goal, we must know the real driving force behind our desires. Especially when what we desire to do or have is noble and good; there is such a thing as *doing the right thing for the wrong reason* **(James 4:3)**. No matter how helpless you may feel at times, never forget that you are never alone in your struggle against sin. If our enemy had his way, he would have us believe that there is no help in our storms and that no one would ever understand our struggles. However, **1 Peter 5:9-10** continues to coach us by saying, *"Stand firm against him [satan] and be strong in your faith. Remember that your family of believers all over the world is going through the same kind of suffering you are. In his kindness God called you to share in his eternal glory by means of Christ Jesus. So after you have suffered a little while,* *he will restore, support, and strengthen you, and he will place you on a firm foundation"* (NLT emphasis added).

Faith is essential because it keeps our focus on the right thing. How we feel about something or someone will affect our judgment. **Proverbs 3:5-6 (NIV)** says, *"Trust in the Lord with all your heart and lean not on your own understanding; in all your ways submit to him, and he will make your paths straight."* When we put our hearts in God's hands, He will keep us secure through our seasons of testing and trial and enable us to stand firm. So as seasons change, hold on to The Lord to anchor your soul. Take note of the *"wise builder"* Jesus talks about in **Matthew 7:24-27**; It's never a matter of *"IF"* our trial will come, but a matter of *"WHEN."* We must always strive to be anchored in God and never forfeit to the enemy an "opportune time."

"Beloved, think it not strange concerning the fiery trial which is to try you, as though some strange thing happened unto you: But rejoice, inasmuch as ye are partakers of Christ's sufferings; that, when his glory shall be revealed, ye may be glad also with exceeding joy."
1 Peter 4:12-13 KJV

Heavenly Father, forgive me for my transgressions as I forgive those who have transgressed against me. Lead me away from the things that tempt me, and deliver me from the schemes of the evil one. In Jesus' name, Amen.

TWENTY

A HEART TO ENDURE

JAMES 5:11

Indeed we count them blessed who endure. You have heard of the perse-
verance of Job and seen the end intended by the Lord—that the Lord is
very compassionate and merciful. (James 5:11 NKJV)

My twelfth-grade English teacher Mrs. Moore taught me a lesson that forever
blessed me naturally and spiritually. Graduation was a time full of excitement,
stress, and anxiety for us all. At the time, like many of my peers, I was taking the
SAT exam. It was the final piece of my academic portfolio to help determine my
college acceptance and scholarship money eligibility.

After taking the practice exam, I lamented to Mrs. Moore about how long the
test was. During the exam, a fellow tester had fallen asleep through two entire
sections before being startled awake by the proctor's announcement, "Time,
pencils down!" He continued testing remorsefully through the following sections. I will never forget hearing his subsequent sighs and moans as he continued. He knew that his chances of a decent score were lost. Mrs. Moore sharply
interrupted my complaining. Refusing to allow negative self-talk to cripple her
students, Mrs. Moore sharply responded. "Saddi, you must realize that TIME

is part of the test." She enlightened me further, explaining how *concentration* is measured as a factor, in part, to determine a person's overall intelligence capacity. In like manner, the ability to endure is partly a measure of our faith capacity.

Hebrews 6:19 NKJV
"This hope we have as an anchor of the soul, a hope both sure and steadfast and one which enters within the veil,"

In writing to the church at Ephesus, Paul prays that God grants the believers the spirit of wisdom and understanding *(Ephesians 1:17-18)* so that they would be clear on what God has called them to do; a prayer we would do well to repeat ourselves. When it comes to life and purpose, it is not enough to know *what* to do. We must also know *"when"* in order to benefit from God's timing. Faith requires work; depending on the season, the work that is required may mean simply standing still *(Ephesians 6:13)*. Standing still sounds counterintuitive in our fast-paced world. The concept of *"perfect timing"* is more closely attributed to speed than patience. Joseph "the dreamer" *(Genesis 37)* is a famous portrait of God choosing a young man in his youth to be destined for great things. While Joseph had his share of haters, cheaters, and misfortunes, God was always with him. His purpose was made possible only by his ability to endure the undesirable seasons of his journey. **Psalms 105:19 NLT** says, *"Until the time came to fulfill his dreams, the Lord tested Joseph's character."*

Time

Character is proven over time. Our hope for the future anchors our souls and comforts us with God's presence. God is with us and accessible to us for strength, reassurance, and direction *(Hebrews 4:16)*. Philippians 3:10 NKJV says, *"That I may know Him and the power of His resurrection, and the fellowship of His sufferings, being conformed to His death."* The depth of "knowing" Paul declares here is far from shallow. As in any relationship, specific depths of intimacy can only be unlocked under certain conditions. Oddly enough, Paul related "fellowship with the Lord" closer to the experience of suffering than victories. This "fellowship of suffering" is an experience reserved for a particular group, similar to the "immediate family list" a hospital would use to manage a patient's visiting hours. If a patient's health permits, any friend or associate could come during visiting hours when the patient "is rested, in good spirits, with plenty of help nearby. However, those on the "immediate family list" are allowed beyond visiting hours in dyer times. While the doctor is away, this intimate group provides mental and emotional support, from holding hands to singing in the loved one's ear. Even though they can do nothing to stop the pain, their presence makes the trial bearable for the patient. Fellowship in suffering may not sound enjoyable, but those engaged in this type of fellowship will find such moments unforgettable and their bond unbreakable. Life is capable of providing us all with moments of crisis where such a list will be needed for us personally, or we may be called upon to provide comfort for another. Whatever you do in such times of need, never forget that Jesus is there. He promised an unbreakable fellowship with those that trust Him. He is the friend that sticks closer than a brother and will always be with us, even until the end of the world *(Matthew 28:20).*

> **2 Peter 3:17 NIV**
> **"Therefore, dear friends, since you have been forewarned, be on your guard so that you may not be carried away by the error of the lawless and fall from your secure position."**

Pain

Psalms 19 celebrates the immense value and utility of God's word. Psalms 19 describes the attributes of scripture using descriptive words such as beauty, tremendous value, peace, and wisdom. Among these superlatives, *"informant"* can also be added. Psalms 19:11 NKJV says, *"Moreover by them (God's word) Your servant is warned, And in keeping them there is great reward"* (emphasis added). **God's word comforts us for the future, especially when that future is uncomfortable.** God helps us endure by preparing our hearts for a coming storm.

By a word of wisdom, God began Mary's 33-year heart preparation to endure her son's crucifixion *(Luke 2:35)*. It was Jesus' words of prayer that preserved Peter from backsliding to recovery after denying his Lord *(Luke 22:31-32)* and later how he was meant to die *(John 21:19)*. God isn't always so blunt, he knows just what to say to each of us, how to say it and what we can handle. God's word is meant to strengthen and encourage us, not scare us. That's why we are best prepared for future trials by responding to what God requires of us today. The daily bread God has designed for your strengthing may come in a song sent to you by a friend, a sermon you're about to hear, or a hug a loved one is compelled to give you.

Persuasions

2 Peter 3:17 refers to the danger of being *"carried away"* into error due to being *"unprincipled ."* Being *carried away* is essential to note because those who are typically successful, regardless of their field of specialty, share the trait of being deeply principled in what they do. Principles guide our convictions. Convictions form the principles we live our lives by and the wisdom we decide to listen to when making decisions. Principles are powerful because they are not easily broken. Natural laws like inertia, friction, momentum, kinetic energy, and gravity are principles of physics we depend on to build our civilization's infrastructure. Tragically, principals can be ignored but not without serious consequences. An engineer who cheats on building codes to increase his profits is no safer than the child of God who cheats their faith to make a few important friends. Principles provide safety and longevity when they are honored. As it is in the natural, so it is in the spiritual. Abiding by the spiritual principles

of love, joy, peace, patience, kindness, goodness, faithfulness, gentleness, and self-control *(Galatians 5:23-24)*, we build lives tempered for storms, full of fruit, and trusted by others.

Be encouraged that God grants the faith to finish. The race is not given to the quick-witted or the strong-willed but to those with hearts set to endure until the end *(Matthew 24:13)*. Come what may, be fully persuaded, and hold fast to your confession of faith. Hold fast to the gifts and goals you have been granted and fulfill the purpose you've been created to accomplish. Perhaps you do not fear being dissuaded; let me encourage you not to delay either. Procrastination is as devastating as sabotage; to ensure that we run our race at the right pace, the Lord sometimes allows pressure to pursue us just so that we maintain our sense of urgency. Complacency brings with it the tendency to fall asleep at the wheel while taking tomorrow for granted. It's not enough to start well but to finish strong. There is no way around endurance but to persevere. Jesus said, "In your patience [endurance] possess ye your souls" *(Luke 21:19 KJV) [emphasis added]*. Whatever you have set your heart to do, whatever dream has been placed in your heart, it is your duty to walk in it. In the meantime, embrace the challenge the test of time brings. It may feel like you are getting punished; however, in time, you will find that you are being proven.

"May the Lord direct your hearts into the love of God and into the steadfastness of Christ."
2 Thessalonians 3:5 ESV

Heavenly Father, when I encounter the struggles that strain the fabric of my soul, wrap me in your arms. Remind me of your presence when I lose the words to pray. When I have done all to stand, help me to endure without giving up so that I can witness the salvation of your plan. Despite how I feel now, I know this pain is nothing compared to the Glory You will later reveal. In Jesus' name, Amen.

TWENTY-ONE

A RIGHTEOUS REWARD

1 CORINTHIANS 15:58

Therefore, my beloved brethren, be steadfast, immovable, always abounding in the work of the Lord, knowing that your toil is not in vain in the Lord. (1 Corinthians 15:58 NKJV)

Nothing fuels our endurance quite like hopeful expectations. God made us both goal and reward oriented, and it pleases Him to bless us greatly. After all, through Christ, God has blessed us with a covenant full of *"better promises"* **(Hebrews 8:6)**, ensuring an abundant life found in Jesus. What is equally true is our need to be reminded of His rewards *(Psalm 103:2)*. No one is immune to being swept away by the hustle and bustle of the day's duties and the grind of passing years. God knows how easy it is for us to lose our way, so He echoes His word throughout scripture as a father does his child. God desires that we live a life full of purpose, considering every choice we make with eternity in view. I Corinthians 9:24 refers to life as a race, with a prize reserved for the winner at the end. The apostle Paul continues with his encouragement to us, saying that we must *"run to win."*

It is not enough for us to live but to thrive. It's not enough for a partici-
pant to merely be in the race but to win it! Achieving what we have declared
to accomplish from the beginning is the crown of any endeavor. In Psalms
90:12 (KJV), we find a prayer that Moses prayed: *"So teach us to number our
days, That we may apply our hearts unto wisdom."* In essence, Moses asked for
God's help in ensuring that his life's focus aligned with his life's purpose. To put
it in *"race terms,"* Moses asked God to point him in the right direction and set
the appropriate pace for victory. From our perspective, we don't know if our
lives will be a marathon or a sprint; be it 80 years or 18. Whatever the length
of time He's assigned, God will call us to account for how we've used it. While
marathons and sprints are both races, each has a different approach to the use of
time. That is why vision is essential; it gives us our "why" and *"reason"* to press
ahead. Time dictates the pace we must keep to complete the journey despite
how we feel or what season we are in **(Proverbs 29:18).** David said it like this, *"I
had fainted, Unless I had believed to see the goodness of the LORD in the land of
the living. Wait on the LORD: Be of good courage, and he shall strengthen thine
heart: wait, I say, on the LORD."* **(Psalm 27:13-14 KJV).**

Galatians 6:9 KJV
*"And let us not be weary in well doing: for in due season
we shall reap, if we faint not."*

With every measure of faith, we must fight not to faint! Whether standing
in a dry place like David in Psalm 27 or struggling to serve as described in
Galatians 6:9, beware of weariness - it always comes before fainting. Weariness
is a subtle saboteur not to be confused with physical fatigue. Its effects are not
readily seen externally but will eventually manifest if left ignored. Life and labor
are exhausting; God understands this and has already scheduled our times of
refreshing with promises of replenishment for those who endure hardness as
good soldiers **(Psalms 23:3, II Timothy 2:3).** It is a great paradox that we
must rest in Him, while on the battlefield of faith. We will find our strength is

adequate to endure trials, when we rely on God's grace instead of our grit. This "*rest*" is trust, rooted in love. There is nothing more indomitable than love, for God is love **(1 John 4:8)**, and love can endure anything **(1 Corinthians 13:7)**. Love must be emphasized because weariness is a symptom that occurs when love leaves.

Consider a retired Olympic runner dedicated to running ten miles a day. Of course, it keeps him in great shape, and he enjoys the time he gets to think while on the trail, but the runner runs because he loves it. His body may not always agree to get up at 5 am, but he soldiers on. Often he fights the temptation to cut the run short, thinking perhaps eight miles is as good as ten; instead, he pushes through. Exhausted with legs burning and back tight, he makes it home, kicks off his shoes, and lays on the floor. After seeing him stumble in, his neighbor calls to know if he is alright. The runner responds to his neighbor, telling him he is exhausted from running ten hard miles. When the neighbor asks what he will be up to tomorrow, the runner replies with a smile; *"Running"!* Even while lying on his back, tired from his last ten miles, he looked forward to tomorrow because he's never grown tired "*of*" running. On the other hand, weariness is losing your love for something to the point you're tired "*of it*" instead of "*from it*." Like this runner, we should never fear fatigue but welcome it when it comes, knowing that we will always find rest in Jesus to continue.

Matthew 11:28-29 KJV

"Come unto me, all ye that labour and are heavy laden, and I will give you rest. Take my yoke upon you, and learn of me; for I am meek and lowly in heart: and ye shall find rest unto your souls."

Following Jesus means having solace in knowing that he is Lord over the road of life we travel on. Though He owns the road, we own our responses to life's hills and curves. Parts of our journey sometimes seem longer than others, and rugged terrains may be disproportionate to what we anticipated. It is encouraging to know that God knows every step we take and every choice we must make. God honors our sacrifices and faithfulness. Jesus promises that those who have forsaken all to follow Him will receive a hundredfold return in this life and the life to come **(Matthew 19:29)**. There is great reward in doing life God's way. Psalm 16:11 KJV says, *"Thou wilt shew me the path of life: in thy presence is fulness of joy; at thy right hand there are pleasures for evermore."*

Who can number the countless riches of God's grace toward us? Even more fascinating is how God's blessings are as unique as we are—perfectly tailored to our needs, our build, and our purpose. God doesn't reserve all of His rewards for the end of the race, but dispenses His promises as we travel His path. God's continuous blessings are the secret ingredients to the grace that keeps us going. God gives us peace that surpasses understanding and the discernment that helps us to make sound decisions. He does all this to enable us to finish the race so that he can shower us, yet again, for a job well done. It doesn't matter where we find ourselves in our journey; only that we keep going. The Lord's delight is to pay you handsomely for all the work rendered to the king **(Matthew 20:14-15)**.

"I have fought a good fight, I have finished my course, I have kept the faith: Henceforth there is laid up for me a crown of righteousness, which the Lord, the righteous judge, shall give me at that day: and not to me only, but unto all them also that love his appearing."
<u>*2 Timothy 4:7-8 KJV*</u>

Lord, I thank you for another day to do your will. I pray that you grant me the strength to keep doing what is right. It's sometimes difficult, especially when I don't see if what I have been asked to do is making a difference. Today, grant me the privilege to see in part the fruits of my efforts. Lord, I'm not asking for recognition, I need your confirmation. Be so kind as to show me a "token for good," reminding me that you are truly with me (Psalm 86:17). In Jesus' name, I pray, Amen.

TWENTY-TWO

HOLD FAST YOUR CONFESSION

HEBREWS 10:22-23

Let us draw near with a true heart in full assurance of faith, having our hearts sprinkled from an evil conscience and our bodies washed with pure water. Let us hold fast the confession of our hope without wavering, for He who promised is faithful. (Hebrews 10:22-23 NKJV)

In this life, we will have tribulation *(John 16:33)*, so let us "take heart," not take cover. Life is as unpredictable as God is consistent and reliable. Through our knowledge of Him, our faith is measured by our responses to circumstances, not by the pressures they inflict on us. The writer in Hebrews 10:22 encourages us to draw near to God with a sincere heart, fully assured by our faith in Him, knowing that He is truly worthy of our complete trust. Moreover, our conscience is clear from past mistakes, and our present selves are dedicated to walking in His pure purpose. These reminders are essential as they will serve as our *helmet of salvation,* keeping us assured in faith and a *breastplate of righteousness,* protecting our hearts from an evil conscience.

What an interesting phrase, *"...and having done all, to stand".* Ephesians 6:13 points out that we must play an active role in the successes of our battles. As good soldiers, we set our minds to endure *(2 Timothy 2:3)*, equip ourselves for action, and give all we have, leaving the power to stand ultimately to God. Remember, by God's grace, we have been saved so that no one can boast in their strength *(Ephesians 2:8-9)*. The Lord empowers us to stand beyond our perceived limits so that we may see the salvation of His plan. *"Holding fast to your confession"* means holding tightly without letting go. In so doing, we are sure to encounter fears, disappointments, and challenges along the way, but the race is already won. While our story has been written, we still must live out its pages *(Psalms 139:16)*. In the game of life, our confession is the ball, and any progress made, no matter how impressive or great, counts for nothing if we lose it. My college football coach often screamed, "The ball is the issue!" He hated for us to fumble. He always reminded us that no amount of yards gained or points scored would count unless we retained possession of the ball. Jesus asks, what does it profit a man to gain the whole world and lose his soul *(Mark 8:36)*? *Your confession is the issue.*

Job 2:3-5 NKJV

"Then the Lord said to Satan, "Have you considered My servant Job, that there is none like him on the earth, a blameless and upright man, one who fears God and shuns evil? And still he holds fast to his integrity, although you incited Me against him, to destroy him without cause." 4 So Satan answered the Lord and said, "Skin for skin! Yes, all that a man has he will give for his life. 5 But stretch out Your hand now, and touch his bone and flesh, and he will surely curse You to Your face!"

Revelations 12:1 says that we overcame the enemy by the blood of the lamb (*Christ's sacrifice*) and the word of our testimony (*our confession*). In Job's famous example of faithful endurance under great trial, we gain wisdom for endurance. The consistency he reveals through his character teaches a peculiar truth. In Job's defining season, the object of satan's attack wasn't hidden behind his possessions but hidden in God's character. Though Job suffered a significant loss to his family, wealth, friendships, and personal health, it was Job's confession satan wanted to change! The "*accuser*" sneered at Job's dedication to God as circumstantial appeasement. Thinking there is no way a human could, in their way, return God's unconditional love. What God knew about Job, he knows about us. We stand because we stand in faith in Him. For us to lose trust in what we've learned of God would grieve Him deeply **(Hebrew 10:38)** and leave us vulnerable. We are God's prize possession, as He is ours. Our reward is not in things but in Him, and our victory is in the testimony of our relationship. A simple definition of testimony is "*to say the same as.*" When we testify of God's goodness, we attest that His word is as good in earthly experience as it is in heaven **(Matthew 6:10)**. So, whatever God says about us, we must "*say the same as*" He does, giving God the only say in our lives.

It is good practice to rehearse your confession daily. We live in a world full of contradictions and uncertainty. We are reminded that the visible things are passing away, while the unseen things are eternal *(2 Corinthians 4:18)*. This is what I call *living life with eternity in mind*. We address our daily tasks with one eye on eternity to keep our priorities in proper perspective. Be encouraged, friend; whatever opposition you face, He who has promised is faithful. We do not need to worry; The Good Shepard provides rest, protection, provision, and comfort. Always remember that He is in control. The advisory wants nothing more than for us to go back on our word, change our minds, and deny the Lord that has redeemed us at great cost *(1 Peter 1:18-19)*. Are you less valuable than two sparrows? Your heavenly Father feeds them! Seek God's leadership and his way of doing things, and everything we need will be heaped upon us *(Matthew 6:33)*. So let us ask God for the grace to serve Him in a way that pleases Him, allowing us to stand firm without wavering no matter how hot things become.

Daniel 3:15-18 NKJV
"Now if you are ready at the time you hear the sound

> *of the horn, flute, harp, lyre, and psaltery, in symphony*
> *with all kinds of music, and you fall down and worship*
> *the image which I have made, good! But if you do not*
> *worship, you shall be cast immediately into the midst of*
> *a burning fiery furnace. And who is the god who will*
> *deliver you from my hands?" Shadrach, Meshach, and*
> *Abed-Nego answered and said to the king, "O Nebuchad-*
> *nezzar, we have no need to answer you in this matter. If*
> *that is the case, our God whom we serve is able to deliver*
> *us from the burning fiery furnace, and He will deliver us*
> *from your hand, O king. But if not, let it be known to*
> *you, O king, that we do not serve your gods, nor will we*
> *worship the gold image which you have set up."*

Life can apply pressures we can't always anticipate, challenging our deepest convictions. Having *"the answer"* secured in our hearts before the test begins ensures we stand firm on our day of trial. David concluded that he would *"hide the word of God in his heart"* as a guardrail from falling into bad decisions *(Psalms 119:11)*. In Psalms 119, he continues to declare that God's word is always right concerning ALL things and that any other way would be detestable to him *(vs. 128)*. Bold words like these are often misunderstood as fanatical by those who do not live by faith. The Bible says that those who live by the Spirit's leading are rarely understood *(1 Corinthians 2:15)*. Our confession of faith is like a treasure hidden in a field. Vailed by our bodies, God's heavenly treasure shines through our acts of love and obedience, working for us an outcome more incredible than we could ever imagine, bringing glory to God as the architect of our victorious stand.

Daniel 3:15-18 shows three friends cornered by a king, demanding their submission to an ordinance contrary to their beliefs. This was no hollow threat; they stood to lose more than their livelihoods but their lives. As we read their response, we hear one speak for all without hesitation, without fear, and full of faith. They were trusting their entire lives to God's reputation. They were fully persuaded to be as consistent a witness as The Father of heaven has been their God. Standing firm, they made it known by word and deed that their faith was not conditional but fundamental. Declaring God well able to deliver them if He chose to. Finally, in what sounded like their last will and testament, they said, *"Let it be known to you, O king, that we do not serve your gods, nor will we worship the gold image which you have set up."* These young men had purposed it in their hearts long before they had to face the furnace that their testimony would never change.

Mark 4:22-23 NIV
"For whatever is hidden is meant to be disclosed, and whatever is concealed is meant to be brought out into the open. If anyone has ears to hear, let them hear."

The Daniel account continues, with God showing up miraculously, delivering them from harm, and seeing them promoted to royal jobs. Such intense examples aren't as relatable to our comparatively civilized modern society. However, we are not without examples of those who have lost life or livelihood for the sake of their convictions. The enemy doesn't mind what tool he uses, just as long as our confessions are forfeited. If public pressures can cause a thousand stumbles, then private compromises can cause ten thousand. God testified of King David, describing him as a man after His own heart. It is with our hearts that Hebrews 10:22 encourages us to draw near to God. If there is any threat of us drifting away, it will be in the heart, where symptoms first appear. David is one of the few people in scripture where we see his life played out from the cradle to the grave. In his life as a warrior king, many of his defining moments were fought in private. In David's moral battles, we can find the tools to win in ours. In Psalms 19:12-14 there's a prayer request that I often find helpful. It says, *"...cleanse thou me from secret faults. Keep back thy servant also from presumptuous sins; let them not have dominion over me:"* How dangerous is the sin of <u>presumption</u> to us all?

- David <u>presumed</u> he could stay home while his army was at war, leading him to secretly desire a man's wife and later kill a friend *(1 Kings 15:5).*

- Peter <u>presumed</u> he would have the courage to join Jesus in crucifixion, only to deny him three times under the cloak of disguise while calling down curses *(Matthew 26:73-75).*

- A man named Achan <u>presumed</u> no one would notice him taking some of Jericho's spoils. He secretly hid it in the place he and his family would later be buried for his crimes *(Joshua 7:10-26).*

- Judas <u>presumed</u> 30 pieces of silver was sufficient wage to betray his master secretly *(Matthew 26:14-16).*

Perhaps that's why the psalmist asked for God to cleanse him from secret faults. We must beware of *"heart lies."* Our imaginations can be used to convince ourselves that *"God understands"* when we knowingly do what He warned us to avoid, thinking that He only winks at our secret sins. The curious thing about "secret *sins"* is that they significantly affect our conscience. Private failures bring with them a weight of shame that rob us of holy boldness and courage of character. Admitting them openly is a struggle when pride pressures us to clinch the portrait we want others to have of us. Take heart, friend; remember there is no temptation on planet Earth that is not common to the human condition. You don't need a microphone to confess, just a friend. There is no need to post your mistakes online to align with God's word. Never mind how bad you believe your struggle is; it's not strong enough to stand against your confession of faith. Christ has made us free for love's sake, so *"let the redeemed of the Lord say so."* A sin, un-confessed, is a sin not yet defeated *(James 5:16).*

"Think back on those early days when you first learned about Christ. Remember how you remained faithful even though it meant terrible suffering. Sometimes you were exposed to public ridicule and were beaten, and sometimes you helped others who were suffering the same things. You suffered along with those who were thrown into jail, and when all you owned was taken from you, you accepted it with joy. You knew there were better things waiting for you that will last forever. So do not throw away this confident trust in the Lord. Remember the great reward it brings you! Patient endurance is what you need now, so that you will continue to do God's will. Then you will receive all that he has promised."
Hebrews 10:32-36 NLT

Father, despite what life may bring, you deserve my praise and trust. Though I may not presently see the good working on my behalf, I know your hand is on me. Hold me up. Let my souls live so I may praise you. All the days of my life, I will wait on you for my time of rescue. In Jesus' name, Amen.

TWENTY-THREE

THEY THAT WAIT

ISAIAH 40:29-31

"He giveth power to the faint; and to them that have no might he increaseth strength. Even the youths shall faint and be weary, and the young men shall utterly fall: but they that wait upon the LORD shall renew their strength; they shall mount up with wings as eagles; they shall run, and not be weary; and they shall walk, and not faint." (Isaiah 40:29-31 KJV)

Proverbs 25:11 says, *"A word fitly spoken is like apples of gold in pictures of silver."* How wonderful it is when God fitly speaks to us amid trials? God's fitly spoken words are needed most when we stand between hearing the promise and holding the promise. These are the midnights before the morning times, the *"meantimes"* between our good times. In these moments, God fits in a word worthy of our memory and essential to our endurance.

Isaiah Chapter 40 carries within it the saving Gospel of God. The *"good news"* declares and describes how God saves his people. God's established plan to save us existed long before our problems began. Being God, He sometimes exercises the prerogative not to reveal the *"when"* of our deliverance. I've heard patience described as one's ability to keep hopeful expectations after the determined delivery time has come and gone. In my experience, the sweetest victories seemed to have come after a period in which my endurance was tested to new lengths. I've grown to affectionately recognize such victories as *"The Win After, The When"!* When we patiently endure, God endows us with the grace to stand beyond our limits in accordance with His perfect plan *(2 Corinthians 12: 8-9)*. Growing tired, weary, or even heavy-hearted is not a sin. What determines the success or failure of our endurance is our willingness to be utterly dependent on God.

> **Lamentations 3:25-26 (KJV)**
> *"The Lord is good unto them that wait for him, to the soul that seeketh him. It is good that a man should both hope and quietly wait for the salvation of the Lord."*

They that *"wait"* on the Lord, *"depend"* on the Lord. Waiting on the Lord is not passive but intentionally leaning on His strength. A willing and ready person depends on Him daily, moment by moment living by the grace His daily bread provides. We risk fatigue of the heart when our worries extend beyond today into tomorrow's circumstances that may or may not be. God's grace is sufficient for today's uncertainty. Using today's grace for another day's challenge is *frustration personified*. Our Lord said in Matthew 6:34, *"Take therefore no thought for the morrow: for the morrow shall take thought for the things of itself. Sufficient unto the day is the evil thereof."* We can take on the challenges of the day without fear of stumbling, knowing God has provided His grace to stand *(Romans 5:17)*.

Dependence on God is an act of courage produced by faith. Though times often change, we know that God never does. His consistency warrants our trust. In Him, we are able to stand by what He says, despite what we see. Never forget - God loves us, although present pains suggest otherwise. God fully understands our needs, anxieties, and desires as The Good Shepherd. He positions us in these *"meantime"* trials to bring to life the things we couldn't imagine for ourselves *(1 Corinthians 2:9)*. What's more impressive than this, is what God accomplishes in us during our waiting time. Something miraculous occurs in us which can only be achieved in our waiting.

More than mere maturing, we are transformed while in the cocoon of our trials. Isaiah 40 describes the believer who successfully waits on the Lord, mounting up on wings as an eagle. This transformation empowers the believer to travel with new speed and efficiency. These *"spiritual wings"* enables the runner to continue towards their destiny with a newfound love for running. The believer continues their walk of faith soaring above the doubts that once debilitated them through stumbling. Only in such experiences are we transformed. As the Apostle Paul understood, he welcomed good and bad experiences. Such experiences required him to press on until his transformation was complete *(Philippines 3:9-15)*.

The Lord is good to those who depend on Him and the soul that seeks after Him *(Lamentations 3:25)*. God is good, even when life is not. God is good; even when his hand seems heavy upon us, He is our Father! One of my favorite scriptures is Jeremiah 29:11. God reaffirms His love for His people and *His intentions* to bring them to their desired place of promise. However, this scripture is a *"meantime"* word. At this point, Israel is being driven out of their land into captivity in Babylon. God preserves their land from misuse while purging them in the *"meantime"* from the forgetfulness that caused them to abandon their dependency on Him.

When calamity or disappointment hits our lives, it is only natural to ask God "WHY," wondering if we were somehow deserving or if God has since changed His mind concerning His love for us. Knowing our tendency for this, God always sends a *"meantime"* word to answer the questions we are sometimes afraid to ask. In case there is any doubt, God doesn't mind stating plainly that He still loves you *(Jeremiah 31:3)*. The Lord thinks the world of you *(Psalms*

17:8), but in the *"meantime,"* we must trust that a beautiful transformation is taking place during some of our darkest hours.

> ### Psalm 130:5-6 (KJV)
> *"I wait for the Lord, my soul doth wait, and in his word do I hope. My soul waiteth for the Lord more than they that watch for the morning: I say, more than they that watch for the morning."*

We do not live by bread alone but by every word that comes from the mouth of God *(Matthew 4:4)*. We do not make it through tough times by friends alone, but by the *"meantime"* words He speaks to us along the way. Jesus said His words are spirit, and they are life *(John 6:63)*. By faith; we understand that everything was made possible by God's word. The same is true for the strength we need to endure difficult times *(Psalm 119:107)*. The Psalmist says that he depends on the Lord more than those who rely on the sun to rise! To sincerely say such a thing is not to give way to poetic superlative, but to confess a conviction born out of hard times successfully endured. In the darkest of times, waiting involves bouts with doubt, the temptation to close window blinds along with our hearts, and the pressure to allow our praise to fall silent.

Psalm 27:14 KJV says, *"Wait on the Lord: be of good courage, and he shall strengthen thine heart: wait, I say, on the Lord."* I will be the first to admit that waiting takes courage. We will only know how we will respond once we are tested. Our personal "Red Sea" experiences will test our resolve while the enemy of our testimony remains in hot pursuit. Rest assured that the command remains the same, stand still, and see the salvation of the Lord. In doing so, we leave the task of saving to God, while He leaves us the task of trusting. Jesus said, *"By standing firm, you will win your souls"* *(Luke 21:19 NLT)*.

If we can trust God with our anxieties, fears, and insecurities, He will show himself mighty and strong on our behalf, bringing us through our trials better than before. Our victorious transformation depends on our ability to wait. Waiting can be incredibly difficult when God's timing does not fit our own *(Isaiah 55:8-9, Ecclesiastes 8:6)*. Only God knows *"when"* to deliver the *"Win."* No matter how difficult things become, those who call on the name of the Lord will never be put to shame *(Romans 10:11)*. So stand firm, knowing that God is willing and able to bring you through this and every trial, just as he's done in the past. Our miraculous change and glorious transformation are on the other side of our waiting.

"Ensure your servant's well-being; do not let the arrogant oppress me. My eyes fail, looking for your salvation, looking for your righteous promise. Deal with your servant according to your love and teach me your decrees. I am your servant; give me discernment that I may understand your statutes. <u>It is time for you to act, Lord;</u> your law is being broken. Because I love your commands more than gold, more than pure gold,"
<u>**Psalm 119:122-127 (NIV)**</u>

Father, thank you for being so faithful. You are my present help in time of need. You are my fortress for trouble and my resort for refreshment. Thank you for confirming your love for me and showing me that there is a future you're preparing me for. Thank you for the peace you provide every night and the mercy I awake to every morning. Something incredible is happening. Because of Your word, I don't require my eyes to see it to know it's there. Thank You, In Jesus' name, Amen.

TWENTY-FOUR

THEY THAT THIRST

MATTHEW 5:6

"Blessed are those who hunger and thirst for righteousness, For they shall be filled." (Matthew 5:6 KJV)

Whoever comes to God must believe that He is God and that He is a rewarder of those that diligently seek Him **(Hebrews 11:6)**. Perhaps you have never thought deeply about this, but your love and interest in God reflect His love and interest in you *(John 6:44)*. There are no coincidences when it comes to love; for it to be so, it has to be intentional. Jesus declared to his disciples, *"You have not chosen me, but it is I who have chosen you"* **(John 15:16)**.

God is graciously versatile in how He expresses his desire for us. He uniquely relates to each one of us in the way we best understand. The Psalms say that God makes full use of everyday nature to display his unseen majesty. He goes on to say that the whole earth is filled with God's glory and that the sun, moon, and stars declare his handy work *(Psalm 19:1-14)*. As awesome as that may be, the onslaught of everyday life's obligations and responsibilities can press in on us, stifling our desire to reach higher to answer His divine invitation.

Have you ever been intimidated by the thought of getting to know God better? We may assume that God is too high, or far off for an individual audience with someone like you or I. On the contrary, His word declares that He is not far off but very near to each of us *(Romans 10:8-9)*. Imposter syndrome sets in yet again, even when we are sure that we are His children. Never forget that you are part of that chosen generation and peculiar people, Peter talks about *(1 Peter 2:9)*. Even angels are amazed by the place of privilege God holds for us in His heart *(Job 7:17, Psalm 144:3)!*

When the scriptures speak of *"the deep calling unto deep" (Psalm 42:7-8)* it's describing in part, God matching our desire for Him with a greater desire for us. To thirst for a deeper relationship with God is a blessed position to be in, because that is a prayer He is inclined to respond quickly to. As the deer pants after the water brook, so should our hearts thirst for God *(Psalm 42:1-2)*. Consider yourself blessed when you perceive how *"parched"* you are for His presence. Thanks to this awareness, we develop the boldness to ask for a fellowship that will produce a healthy spring of living water.

John 4:10, 13-14 (NKJV)

"Jesus answered and said to her, "If you knew the gift of God, and who it is who says to you, 'Give Me a drink,' you would have asked Him, and He would have given you living water." Jesus answered and said to her, "Whoever drinks of this water will thirst again, but whoever drinks of the water that I shall give him will never thirst. But the water that I shall give him will become in him a fountain of water springing up into everlasting life."

Sometimes God will personally engage with us in a way that stirs our desire for Him. As our Father and Source, nothing pleases Him more than to be our supply for life. God built into us a dependency that only He can fulfill. Just as cars run on gas, our bodies run on food, and our souls run on God. Jesus met the woman at the well, displaying the heart of the creator, longing to bless her; with the words, *"If you only knew."* When we embrace God's words, it becomes a spring of life to anyone who can perceive its value *(Proverbs 4:13).* Only a genuine and sincere heart is capable of benefiting from the wellspring of God's word *(Psalms 51:17)*. In like manner, Jesus pleads with us in the spirit of Isaiah 55:1 (KJV), saying, *"Ho, every one that thirsteth, come ye to the waters, and he that hath no money; come ye, buy, and eat; yea, come, buy wine and milk without money and without price."*

Psalm 107:36-37 KJV
"He turneth the wilderness into a standing water, And dry ground into watersprings. And there he maketh the hungry To dwell, that they may prepare a city for habitation;"

Blessed indeed are the hungry and thirsty, as the Savior had said. We are not blessed because we stand in need of Him *(the entire world does);* but because our hearts stand ready to receive His promise. God doesn't insist His way upon us *(1Corinthians 13:4-5)*, but He invites us to fellowship by knocking on the doors of our hearts with the hope of sharing with us His heavenly food and drink *(Revelations 3:20)*. In Psalm 27:7-9 we hear the psalmist describe this invitation and response by saying, *"When thou saidst, Seek ye my face; my heart said unto thee, Thy face, LORD, will I seek. Hide not thy face far from me".*

Sometimes, God's invitations lead us to places of solitude for stretching. God led the children of Israel into a wilderness to better learn His voice and ways before leading them into their place of promise. Though difficult and scary, hindsight shows the wisdom behind this *"meantime"* period in which God trains us to rely on Him. This training period teaches us how to receive His water in seasons of dryness. God is doing more than keeping us in His special care during this time; He is helping us better understand *WHO* is sustaining us. During the Exodus experience, the children of Israel were given *"manna"* to eat, clothes and shoes that grew with them which never wore out; and drank water that flowed out of a rock! 1 Corinthians 10:1,3-4 explains it this way, *"For I do not want you to be ignorant of the fact, brothers and sisters, that our ancestors were all under the cloud and that they all passed through the sea. They all ate the same spiritual food and drank the same spiritual drink; for they drank from the spiritual rock that accompanied them, and that rock was Christ"* (NIV). This holy thirst drives our eyes from looking inward to upward. The blessing of this godly thirst is that, it is God for whom we thirst after!

A few generations later, Jesus was led by the Holy Spirit into that same desert. Coming off of a 40-day fast, He, too, was hungry *(Matthew 4:1-11)*. Though much can be learned from his testing time, one thing was established; only God can supply our needs and grant our dreams. Blessed are those who hunger and thirst for righteousness because you will have it! James 1:5 (NLT) says, *"If you need wisdom, ask our generous God, and he will give it to you. He will not rebuke you for asking"*. Jesus emerged from His wilderness season in the *"power of the Holy Spirit."* We, too, require a fill-up of God's grace before entering our seasons of fulfillment.

In dry seasons, God's grace is supplied as a miracle of necessity. *In seasons of abundance, God's grace is available upon request, so don't forget to ask.* That is why God warns us not to forget Him once our immediate comforts are met, and we lose sight of how we got there *(Deuteronomy 8:11-14)*. Wisdom is the principal thing; therefore, we must get wisdom, and, in all our thirsting, we must thirst for understanding. As the disciples asked Jesus to teach them to pray, we must take this posture as we meet with Jesus at the well. We must ask him to lead us to drink so that we may never thirst again, Teach us to drink so we will never forget again. Teach us to drink so that we will never lose trust again. Blessed are they that respond to their thirst and dedicate their time to drinking from the rock that is Christ.

"And the Lord will continually guide you, And satisfy your desire in scorched places, And give strength to your bones; And you will be like a watered garden, And like a spring of water whose waters do not fail."
Isaiah 58:11

Lord, I desire to know your heart on the matters of my life. I consider your word right concerning all things. Your word is pure, proven, and trustworthy; that's why I love it so much. Open the eyes of my heart so that I may have your understanding. Teach me your ways. Help me to value your word more than wealth. When I read your word, make it so that the truth you have for me will leap from the page and graft to my heart. Strengthen me to apply your word to my life and family so I may grow by it daily. In Jesus' name, Amen.

TWENTY-FIVE

HE WHO HAS AN EAR TO HEAR

MARK 4:9

And he said unto them, He that hath ears to hear, let him hear. (Mark 4:9 KJV)

Our previous chapter reveals how God ignites our desire to know Him. How, then, can we ignore such a great salvation *(Hebrews 2:3)* when the Lord calls out to us individually to share his heart? We hear God's voice in our hearts through His word and in the echoed testimonies of others who have responded to the Holy Spirit's invitations of fellowship. When Jesus speaks of those with *"ears to hear,"* He refers to those with hearts that desire to understand Him. Hearing God is a sweet privilege, available to every sincere disciple. His voice is not a rare epiphany reserved for clergy but a familiar tone to all who have drawn near to Him.

Because of Christ, we have peace with God, united with Him in right-relationship **(Romans 5:1).** As it is in any relationship, God desires to relate to us. Sin caused humanity's initial relationship to be severed with God, one in which Adam could enjoy a father-son relationship *(Genesis 3:8)*. Abraham was regarded as God's friend *(Isaiah 41:8)*. Enoch had a relationship so close that he was known as the man who walked with God *(Genesis 5:24)*. David captivated God's heart unlike anyone had before *(Acts 13:22)*. John was known as the one whom Jesus loved *(John 21:20-21)*. Can you see the pattern? God wants to commune with us. Our relationship with God means everything to Him.

God is not offended by the fact that we will encounter times when we may question His love for us. Instead, he made provision for our forgetfulness, sending us the Comforter, The Holy Spirit, to remind us at the right time everything God has promised us *(John 14:26)*. The good news God brings recognizes that we need to be led, rather than given a law. This is why God does not depend on a conditional contract of rules sent down for us to follow. Instead, Christ came to establish a covenant of fellowship with each of us, a relationship built on mercy and truth.

A relationship is what God desires, not religion. To be clear, God wants to bring us into an authentic experience with Him. Through our relationship with God, we can effortlessly display what people call "religious *ideals*" in our daily lives. Jesus calls these tangible displays the "fruit of the spirit" *(Galatians 5:22-23)*, which develops over time, yielding to God's instruction day by day. Does that sound too fantastic to be true? Jesus said, "*All those who hear the truth, hear my voice*" *(John 18:37)*. Hearing from the Lord is your right and privilege; experiencing His leading is simply a matter of position, proximity, and discernment.

Position

> *Mark 1:35 KJV*
> *Now in the morning, having risen a long while before daylight, He went out and departed to a solitary place; and there He prayed.*

It's hard to hear God when the busyness of the day and the demands of life dominate our focus and time. Jesus uses the benefit of solitude to carve out dedicated time to talk to the Father before the day begins. It's hard to break away from the cries of the day, but it's necessary to position our hearts to receive the day's instructions. Jesus couldn't stay away for long before his disciples came looking for Him. This reminds us how useful the silent feature on our phones can be in protecting our quiet time. No matter how important we may be to others, we cannot be who they need us to be if we do not first position ourselves to hear God.

In Mark 1:37, we see Jesus emerge from His time of solitude with the Father having plans for the day. There is a certain level of clarity that privacy provides. Not to be confused with loneliness, the solitude of the kind Jesus demonstrates was exclusively spent with the Father. It feels a little unnatural at first; after all, prayer is supernatural work. We must resist the urge to fill the empty quiet with sounds, phone chimes, and background noise. I often find low-playing worship or instrumental music helpful in bringing my heart to a place of worship before prayer, but I'm careful not to lean on such aids as a dependency.

A quiet heart is a waiting heart, and a waiting heart is a listening heart. Proverbs 3:5-6 NLT says, *"Trust in the Lord with all your heart; do not depend on your own understanding. Seek his will in all you do, and he will show you which path to take."* As we grow in understanding prayer, we treasure it as a two-way conversation, not just a time of confession and petition. Believe in the promise of Proverbs 3:6; *God will show us the path to take* if we listen. The solitary place of prayer is not lonely; God is there and wishes to show us things we do not know *(John 16:13-14)*. Before His darkest hour, Jesus took three disciples to a solitary place to pray. Finding a corner of His own a few feet away, Jesus returned to His disciples after a time to see them asleep. He woke them, asking why they could not watch with Him for at least an hour *(Matthew 26:40)*.

In our case, "falling asleep" in prayer is praying without expecting God to respond. We run through our list of worries and concerns and are quick to rise the moment we are done venting. Jesus encourages His disciples to have faith in the character of God so that we can believe we have received the moment we've prayed *(Mark 11:24)*. So if you believe God answers prayer, take your time and wait for His reply. Just because you may be done talking doesn't mean you are done praying. King Solomon encourages those approaching God to do so with care. Ecclesiastes 5:1-2 (NLT) says, *"As you enter the house of God, keep your ears open and your mouth shut. It is evil to make mindless offerings to God. Don't make rash promises, and don't be hasty in bringing matters before God. After all, God is in heaven, and you are here on earth. So let your words be few."* Jesus echoes this sentiment in Matthew 6:7-8 (NIV) when He says, *"And when you pray, do not keep on babbling like pagans, for they think they will be heard because of their many words. Do not be like them, for your Father knows what you need before you ask him."*

Peter was challenged with an hour of watching and prayer. How beneficial would it be if we worked to give an extra 15 minutes of quiet time in prayer devoted to listening? Doing this will start positioning our hearts to hear, believing God will respond. Take your time, <u>watch, and pray</u> *(Matthew 26:41)*. The answer you are longing to hear is in His presence. The world can wait.

Proximity

Psalm 51:1,8 KJV
"Have mercy upon me, O God, according to thy lovingkindness: according unto the multitude of thy tender mercies blot out my transgressions. Make me to hear joy and gladness; That the bones which thou hast broken may rejoice."

It's hard to hear God when our hearts are far from Him *(Matthew 15:8)*. Sin separates us from God; unrepented Sin builds a dividing wall. In Matthew

5:23-24 of The Message Bible, Jesus challenges us to approach God a certain way. *"This is how I want you to conduct yourself in these matters. If you enter your place of worship and are about to make an offering, you suddenly remember a grudge a friend has against you, abandon your offering, leave immediately, go to this friend and make things right. Then and only then, come back and work things out with God."*

It is no accident that 2 Peter 1:8 correlates the height of spiritual maturity to be synonymous with brotherly kindness and love. Our heavenly relationship parallels our ability to keep and maintain our earthly ones. 1 John 4:20 calls anyone who declares their love for God while harboring hate for their fellow man a liar. He says, "That person doesn't know God at all!" 1 Peter 3:7 admonished husbands to treat their wives kindly, or else they risk their prayers being unheard. Relationships matter to God because He uses them more often to speak to us than He does by sending His voice from heaven. As we mature in managing relationships, we will grow in obtaining favor from God and people. After all, God will only forgive our trespasses to the degree we forgive those who trespass against us *(Matthew 6:15)*.

Forgiveness is vital to living in God's will. If we are to receive forgiveness, we must give forgiveness. If we want His will to be done on earth as it is in Heaven, then we must do what He has done from Heaven on earth: forgive. Only clean hands and pure hearts can approach God's holy hill *(Psalm 24:4-5)*. Notice the requirement is *clean hands*, not perfect ones. We all get it wrong sometimes, but Jesus gives us the ownership to make things right. We position ourselves in "right relationship" to hear from God when we forgive. This may be why Jesus uses the scenario in which someone may have a grudge against us.

Putting ourselves in someone else's shoes forces self-examination because *self-righteousness is* more concerned with *looking right* than doing right. Pride creates blind spots in our hearts, making reconciliation difficult. We convince ourselves that the *"other person"* has somehow *"misinterpreted"* our best intentions. Jesus asks that we get it right by seeking forgiveness or by giving it.

Until we do, we will hear nothing more until the command of forgiveness is obeyed.

He that covereth his sins shall not prosper: but whoso confesseth and forsaketh them shall have mercy. (Proverbs 28:13)

The same happened with David when crossed examined by the prophet, Nathan. Nathan helped David take ownership of the wrong he had committed secretly by confronting him with the pain his actions had caused *(2 Samuel 12:7)*. Thanks to the accountability provided by his earthly relationships, David was saved from his inability to hear God because of the sin in his life. While we are here, I would like to encourage those who may not have or currently see the value in faith communities.

I have friends who, for several reasons, experience apprehension when it comes to joining a church or attending regularly. Many of us grew up in an era when church was mandatory for our household. As we've grown, we've either moved to a new state, started demanding careers, or had disappointing encounters with religious leaders and groups. I acknowledge the sensitivity of this subject, and everyone's situation is different. However difficult, I submit that we shouldn't give up seeking God's guidance on the subject. God provides a unique treasure through the gift of corporate worship and community (church).

Individual Benefit & Purpose:

We do ourselves a disservice when we neglect the gifts God gives us to be successful. Hebrews 10:25 (KJV) says, *"Not forsaking the assembling of ourselves together, as the manner of some is; but exhorting one another: and so much the more, as ye see the day approaching."* Some look at church *gatherings, saying, "I don't need all that."* Peter once disagreed with Jesus openly, confident that His faith was so strong that even if the other disciples fell away, it wouldn't affect him *(Matthew 26:33-35)*. Whether we like it or not, God made us to be interdependent so that we would be a blessing to each other.

Time and life happen to us all, and though you may feel strong today, there will come a time you will need a shoulder to lean on. Equally so, think about the people God wants to bless and encourage by the example of your life. When we don't share the life God has given to us with others, it's like taking your ball and going home. I believe Jesus' heart for those navigating this season is one of compassion and patience. In like manner, Jesus looked at the independent Peter in Luke 22:31-32 and said, *"Simon, Simon, behold, Satan hath desired to have you, that he may sift you as wheat: But I have prayed for thee, that thy faith fail not: and when thou art converted [come back], <u>strengthen thy brethren</u>"* (emphasis added).

The Preached Word:

Personal Bible study and prayer are essential, but God's method of conveying the good news is the preached word. To each his own with the style of preaching and presentation you prefer, but there is no substitute for the preacher. The Bible openly admits that the act of preaching is complete nonsense in the face of conventional wisdom *(1 Corinthians 1:23)*. 1 Corinthians 1:25 says, *"Because the foolishness of God is wiser than men; and the weakness of God is stronger than men."*

There we have it; God does more than we ever could while doing the least. According to *(Romans 10:14-15)* we can regard sincere preachers as heavenly-appointed hearing aids, confirming the word of God in our lives. If we trust and obey God's leading, He will lead us to the church He chooses for us *(1 Corinthians 12:18)*. When we settle in the place God appoints for us, we will receive the directional instruction necessary to apply faith to our daily lives.

Safety of Counsel:

Sin separates us from God, making it hard to hear His voice. A community of believers helps provide the perspective and self-awareness we do not have when striving alone. God knows we are better off when we travel with trusted companions. We help each other from drifting off the path and provide support when we are weary. Hebrews 3:13 (KJV) says, *"But exhort one another daily, while it is called To day; lest any of you be hardened through the deceitfulness of sin.* " Sin is deceitful in the way that it affects our hearts.

Though we all fall and sin daily, we must be careful not to allow the mistakes we make to numb our hearts to the need for forgiveness. Just like Nathan did for David, relationships of accountability make it hard for us to lie to ourselves. A friend is often more likely to notice when we've compromised our character before we are ready to admit it. 1 John 1:7 (NKJV) says, *"But if we walk in the light as He is in the light, <u>we have fellowship with one another,</u> and the blood of Jesus Christ His Son cleanses us from all sin"* (emphasis added).

When convicted, David didn't hesitate to respond to God's chance at recovery. He blazed a trail of model repentance, recorded in Psalms 51. Repentance makes it possible for spiritual hearing to be restored, allowing us to enjoy the sounds of His joy and praise. Like a loving father, when we are disobedient, God's loving voice calls us to return to Him while we are still in earshot. Hebrews 4:6-7 reminds us that even when we mess up, God wants nothing more than to dust us off and put us back on track toward destiny.

The key to God's promises is our willingness to hear Him. Hebrews 4:7 says, *"Today when you hear his voice, don't harden your hearts."* Responding in repentance is the saving grace of a listening ear. ***Don't become discouraged when God finds it necessary for you to hear his voice of correction.*** Let it serve as His affirmation, not condemnation. God corrects those He loves ***(Hebrews 12:6-7)***. Proverbs 3:11-12 in the NKJV says, *"My son, do not despise the chastening of the Lord, Nor detest His correction; For whom the Lord loves He corrects, Just as a father the son in whom he delights."* After showing ourselves faithful in responding to His call of repentance, we unlock God's voice to speak of our future and purpose. That's when listening gets exciting. Remember always that God considers you a favored child. The time may come when His correction may stir our emotions in a way that may make Proverbs 3:11-12 easy to forget and hard to believe.

Discernment

__1 Kings 19:11-13 NKJV__
__Then He said, "Go out, and stand on the mountain before__
__the Lord." And behold, the Lord passed by, and a great__
__and strong wind tore into the mountains and broke the__
__rocks in pieces before the Lord, but the Lord was not in the__
__wind; and after the wind an earthquake, but the Lord__
__was not in the earthquake; and after the earthquake a__
__fire, but the Lord was not in the fire; and after the fire a__
__still small voice. So it was, when Elijah heard it, that he__
__wrapped his face in his mantle and went out and stood__
__in the entrance of the cave. Suddenly a voice came to him,__
__and said, "What are you doing here, Elijah?"__

Hearing the voice of God is so awesome that many of us (*at least initially*) think of it as some spectacular event with hair-raising dramatics. Along the way, I've had to surrender many preconceived notions about God's ways. Taking God out of the box of our imagination is essential to experiencing Him in Spirit and Truth. It doesn't matter how big we dream; our imaginations would sell God short. It doesn't matter how righteous our thoughts are; it's all filthy rags by comparison. Fortunately for us, God has made His character clear to us through the scriptures. Our capacity to receive from God is limited only by the degree to which we perceive God correctly.

1 Kings 19:11-13, Elijah had wandered off the path of faith while in a fierce internal battle with fear, brought on by adversarial threats. When emotions are high, we risk losing discernment and failing to decypher God's message amid our messes. For those intently seeking to hear God's voice, Jesus advises in Luke 8:18 that we must be careful in *"how we hear."* This means we must check our hearts and the source from which we receive instruction. Waiting on the voice of God,

Elijah endured torrents of wind, earthquakes, and fire yet remained unmoved until a still, small voice came to him. *God's voice was described as calm and quiet.*

Why wouldn't God's voice be calm and quiet? After all, He is sovereign and never surprised by our situations. As the author of our story, no situation is beyond His ability to save, and He knows exactly how our stories should end. Listen to how James 3:17 describes God's tone: *"But the wisdom that is from above is first pure, then peaceable, gentle, willing to yield, full of mercy and good fruits, without partiality and without hypocrisy."* In light of scriptures like James 3:17, I've developed the conviction that God's peace is how I discern His direction. Just as Elijah stood facing his fears, we must stand amid our firey earthquakes and keep the peace of God. Life's torrents are what make the peace of God so radiant. God's peace provides us a resolve that surpasses human understanding *(Philippians 4:7)*.

God placed that desire to seek Him and hear Him inside of us; Proverbs 20:12 says, *"The hearing ear and the seeing eye, The Lord has made both of them."* Our ability to hear God's voice is a means of grace that He has granted us for victory. By His voice, God increases our faith *(Romans 10:17)*, fulfills His promises *(Isaiah 55:3)*, and directs our steps *(Proverbs 3:5-6)*. What should we say, then? If God is for us, who can be against us? When we pray, trust to hear Him speak. We will find His voice in scripture, the wisdom of mentors, the encouragement of wise friends, and the peace we find in the time of storm.

"Anyone with ears to hear should listen and understand. But blessed are your eyes, because they see; and your ears, because they hear. I tell you the truth, many prophets and righteous people longed to see what you see, but they didn't see it. And they longed to hear what you hear, but they didn't hear it."
Matthew 13:9, 16-17 NLT

Speak Lord, your servant is listening... In Jesus' Name, Amen.

TWENTY-SIX

BE DOERS, NOT HEARERS ONLY

JAMES 1:22

But don't just listen to God's word. You must do what it says. Otherwise, you are only fooling yourselves. (James 1:22 NLT)

To hear what God requires is one thing; being brave enough to do what He says is another thing entirely. The Bible says that "Abraham believed God, and it was accounted to him for righteousness" *(Genesis 15:6)*. We know that Abraham believed in God because he obeyed God. Because of Jesus, a great treasure is laid up for us. As coheirs with Christ, we are also called to "prove" that which is the good, acceptable, and perfect will of God *(Romans 12:2)*. To prove such a thing will no doubt require faith and personal courage, for persecution is prescribed to anyone who intends to live a life pleasing to God *(2 Timothy 3:12)*.

Today's contemporary trends can make doing the will of God hard to do. Some of God's most remarkable servants have lived out their convictions at significant cost. Some have sacrificed personal safety and other's everyday comforts, and some forfeited worthwhile pursuits for the gospel's sake. The book of James encourages that the Father's will should be our chief aim, not just discussing it. Even worse, a person can presume to do God's will as a cloak to accomplish their own desires. In Luke 6:46-49, the Lord explains that we will ultimately do, what is in our hearts, despite what we profess or claim. Some of the expectations God has for us are harder to do than others. God knows our desires and fears. Just as He dealt with people in the past, Christ lovingly challenges us with the same question. *"Why do you call me Lord but do not do what I tell you?"* By His sacrificial love, Jesus demonstrates His willingness to give His life to those who trust Him.

"Lord" is a legal term used today but is outdated in our modern speech unless used as a spiritual superlative, reading scriptures, or praying. Essentially, "Lord" means owner. The same way we say "landlord" today, describing the owner of an area of land or domicile. The strength of our salvation rests on the reality that God is the Lord of it. He purchased us out from under the service(bondage) of sin, to serve Him, by His Spirit unto everlasting life *(Romans 6:19)*. As a born-again believer, the joy of our salvation is the central source of our strength, enabling us to serve God freely. Sin, on the other hand, is a cruel master. It drives a person to dead works with accomplishments that decay over time *(Proverbs 10:7)*. God, however, doesn't give us burdens; He gives us purpose. He doesn't pay wages; instead, He gives gifts *(Romans 6:23)*. God desires willing workers motivated by gratitude *(Psalm 51:12, 1 John 5:2-4)*.

James 1:25 NIV
"But whoever looks intently into the perfect law that gives freedom, and continues in it—not forgetting what they have heard, but doing it—they will be blessed in what they do."

When people are unsure what to do, they often do nothing or too much. Fear and indecision came into the world when Adam and Eve desired more information instead of God's instruction *(Genesis 3:6)*. The same impulses plague us today. We often choose to define good and evil over pursuing our understanding of God. In 2 Corinthians 1:19-20, Paul, Timothy, and Silvanus proved by their behavior God's will, not a summary of *Do's* and *Don'ts*. They said everything done within God's will is met with a resounding Yes and Amen. James proclaims the same in James 1:25, describing it as the *"perfect law of liberty."* God's grace empowers us to serve Him acceptably *(Hebrews 12:28)*. Having the understanding of what we should do, clears the path of many of the pitfalls we should avoid.

The best state of any relationship is where two parties work to please each other. Simply trying not to upset a person is patronizing. In His perfect law of liberty, God instructs us to do that which we know is right and focus on that *(James 4:17)*. After all, if we pursue the desires of the Spirit, we will have no time to do anything else *(Galatians 5:25)*. It doesn't matter how well a person knows scripture; God wants us to live it out to the best we understand. Trust the Lord to reveal more to you as you continue to walk with Him, but first, put the truth He has already shared with you into practice. In Jame 4:17 (NIV), we read, *"If anyone, then, knows the good they ought to do and doesn't do it, it is sin for them."*

God's law is not one of legalism but liberty. When Christ says that *"the way to life"* is straight and narrow, He is not rigid or restrictive but deliberate and intentional. For our sake, God wants us to fulfill our destiny with as few wrong turns and scars as possible. I believe God is more excited about our future than we are sometimes. God's way is the only sure road to travel, yet the temptation to drift is always there. No student majoring in Computer Science signs up for every class a university offers. The student wouldn't have the time or money to take a course load that expensive and unnecessary.

God's law of liberty is there to make sure that doesn't happen to us. God's purpose frees us from dead works. Dead works aren't about sin; it is anything contrary to your life's purpose. Be it family, career, activism, or philanthropy, if it isn't helping you accomplish what God created you to do, it's just another *elective costing you time and resources.* The quickest route to any destination is a straight line. God's path for us is a straight and narrow one. He wants to ensure we make it through the gate that leads to life *(Matthew 7:13-14)*—the life He created.

Matthew 21:28-31 NLT

"But what do you think about this? A man with two sons told the older boy, 'Son, go out and work in the vineyard today.' The son answered, 'No, I won't go,' but later he changed his mind and went anyway. Then the Father told the other son, 'You go,' and he said, 'Yes, sir, I will.' But he didn't go. "Which of the two obeyed his Father? "They replied, "The first."

Like a good father, God knows that our maturing takes time. We don't always do as we should the first time around. Sometimes we fight against God's nudgings contrary to our better judgment. In such cases, God shows His patience toward us through the gift of time. We may have outright refused His call to service in a particular area, but God remains patient. It's only human to respond with a cringe when God's call involves self-sacrifice. In other cases, we may battle feelings of inadequacy or fear. Full of compassion, God uses time to bring us to maturity and faith. Over time we develop the faith and grace needed for the task. God also redeems the time, preserving opportunities once missed to bring them back in a season of maturity.

In the second chapter of the book of James, we are encouraged to guard ourselves against the temptation of being extraordinarily spiritual without God's practical application. With earnestness, James doesn't want us to be like the son who merely agreed in lip service only to ignore his Father's request. Diligent application is yet another *"straight and narrow"* path we all must walk with God's leading to prevent the error of extremes. Extreme action or inaction is equally damning. James 2:18 (NLT) says, *"Now someone may argue, "Some people have faith; others have good deeds.' But I say, 'How can you show me your faith if you don't have good deeds? I will show you my faith by my good deeds."*

Despite our past responses to God's commands, we still have time to return to His service. As long as we are still breathing, there is still time. While time is on our side, let us use it to change for the better. God has shined His favor upon us by graciously giving us time to respond *(2 Peter 3:9)*.

Philippians 2:13 (NIV)
"for it is God who works in you to will and to act in order to fulfill his good purpose."

What a relief— God requires our partnership, not our performance. We are but branches of Christ in the garden of God. Our job is to stay attached to the root that fuels the growth in our life. Partnering with Jesus *(the true vine)*, we stay healthy and strong enough to hold *(bear)* the results He produces. To "bear" fruit is, in part, what Peter described in 2 Peter 1:4 as being *"partakers of the divine nature,"* giving us everything we need for godly and practical living. Paul expressed this reality frankly in Galation 2:20, attributing the fruitfulness of his life to God in saying, *"I am crucified with Christ: nevertheless I live; yet not I, but Christ liveth in me: and the life which I now live in the flesh I live by the faith of the Son of God, who loved me, and gave himself for me."* (KJV)

The sincere desire to please God and to do His will, is helped by the fact that God initiates and equips us to do so *(Philippians 1:6)*. Faith in God produces incredible courage. Some are called to display unwavering trust like Abraham *(Romans 4:20-21)*, forgiveness in the face of assault like Steven *(Acts 7:59-60)*, or a life of sacrifice in the service of others like Paul *(Philippines 1:21-26)*. To be sure, the meek inherit the Kingdom of God, not the weak *(Mattew 5:5)*. God's strength is not our ability to produce but our willingness to trust. Ephesians 6:10 encourages us, *"Finally, my brethren, be strong in the Lord and in the power of His might." (emphasis added)*

It is surprising how much God demonstrates His faith in us. The trials He allows us to overcome are but one example. The burdens of God are pre-approved, and we are never given tasks beyond our capacity to handle *(1 John 5:3)*. His words remind us that the things God can accomplish through our lives are far greater than we can imagine *(Ephesians 3:20)*. Keeping our eyes on Jesus, we are continually being changed into who God intended us to be from the beginning. *We welcome this transformation, knowing that our actions will be the fruit of who we've become.* We must never forget our dependence on God. Every step taken, every word spoken, and mountain moved is done by His daily supply of grace, which must be requested daily if it is to be given daily *(Matthew 6:11)*.

> *Deuteronomy 31:6 NKJV (Joshua 1:9/Mathew 28:20)*
> *"Be strong and of good courage, do not fear nor be afraid of them; for the Lord your God, He is the One who goes with you. He will not leave you nor forsake you."*

Take a moment to consider what God requires of you. Does it scare you a bit? Perhaps it should. Every task God gives is not a matter of our talent but His trust in us. Anytime God calls us to a new work, it is not because of what we know but what He plans to teach us. The good news here is that you are never alone. From Genesis to Revelation, God speaks of his desire and power to be with us every step of our lives *(Matthew 14:28-29)*. Shortly after I received the burden to write, I had to overcome doubt, timidity, and fear. The Lord encouraged me through a friend months before publishing began. My friend told me that fear must be present for me to have courage. We are not to be driven by sight, feelings, or fears; but by the righteousness, peace, and joy in the Holy Spirit *(Romans 14:17)*.

I desire that we live a life worthy of the calling we have received. Despite your initial responses to God's call, if you're still breathing, you still have time to do what needs to be done. Suppose it has been a while since you've been sure of your purpose. Return to the place where you heard Him last. Do the small things you once neglected; faithfulness in small things will yield big promotions *(Luke 16:10)*. In the Spirit of Ephesians 1:16-19 (NKJV), *"[I] do not cease to give thanks for you, making mention of you in my prayers: that the God of our Lord Jesus Christ, the Father of glory, may give to you the spirit of wisdom and revelation in the knowledge of Him, the eyes of your understanding being enlightened; that you may know what is the hope of His calling, what are the riches of the glory of His inheritance in the saints, and what is the exceeding greatness of His power toward us who believe, according to the working of His mighty power."* [emphasis added]

"Not everyone who says to me, 'Lord, Lord,' will enter the kingdom of heaven, but only the one who does the will of my Father who is in heaven."
<u>Matthew 7:21 NIV</u>

Lord, thank you for speaking to me. Your word fills me with hope and great expectation for the future. Increase my heart to walk in the direction of that future today. Order my steps, words, and thoughts to reflect the heart you are renewing in me. In Jesus name, Amen.

TWENTY-SEVEN

WHOSOEVER WILL

ROMANS 10:11

For the scripture saith, Whosoever believeth on him shall not be ashamed. (Romans 10:11)

I invite you to take a minute to reflect on God's promises for your life. What comes to mind? No promise is too small, none too plentiful. Repeat them aloud and in your mind. Ask yourself, "Since what I declare is true of God, what does that mean for me?" Your answer to this question is the difference between having faith and citing facts. The difference between knowing God's word and taking Him at His word is to answer this question. Facts convey information, while faith carries implications. As we explored in the last chapter, faith will drive us to do what we believe.

The result of a life surrendered to God's care is a life full of promises kept and a pattern of trust that encourages others. David's twenty-third Psalm shows that God leads us by the hand for the sake of *"his name."* When our will becomes His will, so do our outcomes. In all his days as a shepherd, soldier, and King, David confessed that he had never seen those walking with God forsaken by Him nor their children denied reasonable care and supply **(Psalm 37:35)**. Paul exclaims in 2 Corinthians 3:2 that we are "living letters," open for all men to read and to know what the Spirit of God says. God's message of love is made clear by how we live out the words He has written in our hearts. Though our purpose is to show God's praise through our lives **(1 Peter 2:9)**, we are warned to guard our hearts against shame. This is because God's goodness is effectually shown in contrast. As believers, we are to shine as a light to the world and serve as the salt of the earth. The present contrast of today's dark and unsavory times produces countless opportunities for people to read the message of peace and security written in the lives of believers. Jesus was clear that we would face trouble in this life. He desires us to have "H*is peace*," which will keep us focused on our purpose despite momentary afflictions **(John 16:33)**. Romans 8:28 encourages us with a *"peace code."*

"And we know that all things work together for good to them that love God, <u>to them who are the called according to his purpose.</u>" [KJV emphasis added]

The loving believer aligned with God's purpose for their life will never be derailed by affliction but propelled to victory. How encouraging it is to face the day knowing that such promises make life's stumbling blocks into stepping stones, and storms become the accelerators of our sails! We need only to trust and believe.

<u>**John 3:16 (KJV)**</u>
"For God so loved the world, that he gave his only begotten Son, that whosoever believeth in him should not perish, but have everlasting life."

Wherever there is a "whosoever," you can be sure that your name and story can be substituted there. God desires His promises to be freely applied to every believing soul. Receiving God's promises is often easier proclaimed than experienced. God's unconditional love has no earthly equal, so as we encounter the depths of His love, we may need help understanding how to respond appropriately **(Acts 2:36-37)**. In addition to comprehending God's love, we grow in trusting the strength of His hand to keep us from falling *(Jude 24-25)*. Ironically, doing so can sometimes feel as if we are in a free fall. An example of this anxiety is found in Matthew 28:17-18. It reveals the *peculiar apprehension* the heart of a disciple may experience as God stretches the limits of what we believe to be possible. Mathew 28:17-18 says, ***"And when they saw him [Jesus], they worshipped him: but <u>some [disciples] doubted</u>. And Jesus came and spake unto them, saying, All power is given unto me in heaven and in earth."*** [KJV emphasis added]

Take note of two incredible things. One, even a worshiper, can experience doubt. The disciple's doubt is not in Jesus, His words, love, or resurrection per se, but in the personal implications of what that belief means for their lives. ***Believing God for others is simple; believing God for yourself is salvation!*** Remember the father in Mark 9:23-24 who came to Jesus for his child's healing. He had faith in Jesus as a healer, for he had heard He'd healed others, but his son had struggled with an affliction since birth. Turning His gaze away from the boy, Jesus looked at the father. He asked him directly, "Do YOU believe I can do this"? Though the boy's father believed, he confessed he had *"unbelief"* and needed Jesus' help to conquer it.

Secondly, Jesus knows the doubts we struggle with *(Hebrews 4:15)* and is loving enough not to accuse us but to encourage us. Jesus shows great compassion for us by not questioning our sincerity but speaking directly to our weaknesses to provide the trusting strength we need. Just as it was with the disciples in Matthew 28:18, Jesus whispers to us amid our worship and gives the same reassurance. ***"All power is given unto me in heaven and on earth."*** Our past, present, or future concerns do not limit God's power. Jesus' victory at Calvery brings us joy, knowing Christ's power secures our lives here on earth and our place with Him in heaven. You may suffer, as most do, from recurring memories of mistakes and mishaps that have occurred in the past. Your heart shrinks as it cringes at your previous behavior as you wonder, *"Lord, how could you possibly use me?"* Trust God in those moments, and you can expect Him to send His Spirit to comfort your heart with the reply, *"Mightily, my child. Mightily."* **(Roman 8:16)**. Never forget, "All power" is "All" power. Confess and repent, and leave the power cleaning to Him.

1 Corinthians 1:26 KJV
"For ye see your calling, brethren, how that not many wise men after the flesh, not many mighty, not many noble, are called:"

We are saved by God's grace through faith, leaving no room for anyone to boast about the good they do because God has done it all **(Ephesians 2:8-9)**. There is no virtue we possess independent of what God has granted us. Our total dependence on God leaves no room for self-righteousness. The very faith we have to believe in God is a gift from God *(Romans 10:17)*. A miracle occurs through our relationship with Him. We are transformed with a new identity, which qualifies us to be His hands, feet, and mouth to the world around us. Despite what you may think of yourself, God adores and desires you to be a part of His family. In 1 Corinthians 1:26, Paul helps believers shake the habit of self-centeredness and become more God-conscious about their daily lives and accomplishments. In this frame of mind, we do not downplay nor dismiss what we accomplish but praise God all the more for the grace that allows us to do His work. John describes this reality in John 1:16, saying, *"And of his [Christ] fulness have all we received, and grace for grace."* [KJV, emphasis added]

Because of Christ, ALL can benefit from God's grace, but grace here has a double meaning. To be *gracious* is to be thankful; to be *graceful* is to display effortless strength. Let us all rely on Jesus and not our ability, being grateful to God and praising Him for his continuous supply of effortless power. Don't be ashamed of your seemingly low qualifications. What you think disqualifies you makes you God's ideal recruit. What the world thinks of you is unimportant when God plans to shape you. He equips whomever He calls and sustains whoever remains **(John 15:4-8)**. How abundant will life become when we realize God doesn't need our intelligence, strength, friendships, or resources? We know God doesn't need these things because He is the one who gave them to us as gifts! Since He is the original owner of all that is good **(James 1:17)**, let us employ them in our service to Him, having *grace* for **grace** in the Lord who has called us.

"Then Peter said unto them, Repent, and be baptized every one of you in the name of Jesus Christ for the remission of sins, and ye shall receive the gift of the Holy Ghost. For the promise is unto you, and to your children, and to all that are afar off, even as many as the Lord our God shall call."
Acts 2:38-39 KJV

Father, thank you for being patient with me. Today, I surrender my hopes, fears, and plans for the future. I see now that You do not call the equipped. You equip those you call. Use me for Your glory. Transform my heart to yield to the purpose you have created in me. In Jesus' name, Amen.

ABOUT THE AUTHOR

 Saddi Williams is a Christian minister and mentor from Washington, DC. He is a member of Scripture Cathedral Ministries in Landover, MD, and serves on the ministerial staff. Known for his engaging expository speaking style and ability to convey the Word of God in a provoking manner, Saddi has distinguished himself as a voice for the Body of Christ. Distilling over two decades of campus, youth, young adult, and local church ministry, Saddi responds to a need with his inaugural project, *"Growing in Knowing God: A Millenial's Journey in Faith."*

Saddi's life and ministry have faithfully responded to God's promptings. His passion is engaging across cultural and generational lines sharing the gospel of Jesus Christ with sincerity and simplicity.

Learn more at www.saddiwilliams.com.